Private, Hybrid and Public Clouds

New computing models and Best Practices

Marc Israel

Aetheis Publishing
a division of Aetheis Ltd

Private, Hybrid and Public Clouds

This book is licensed for your personal use only. This book may not be resold or given away to other people. If you are reading this book and did not purchase it, or it was not purchased for your use only, then you should return it and purchase your copy. Thank you for respecting the work of the author.

Visit the book companion website hybridcloud.business

ISBN: 9781981094196

Imprint: Independently published

You can reach the author at marc.israel@aetheis.com

Table of Contents

Introduction

"Space, the final frontier. These are the voyagers of the
Starship Enterprise. Its five years mission, to explore strange
new worlds, to seek out new life, and new civilizations.
To boldly go where no man has gone before."

Star Trek Series opening

The cloud is not a fashion that appeared by chance, at the turn of scientific discovery. First, because scientific discovery is the fruit of years of research, error, and reflection. Then, because without internet, there would be no cloud. Just like without Arpanet[1], there would never have been the Internet. The cloud is not the latest technology everyone is talking about. It is the ultimate result of powerful technological, commercial and human forces.

Like wealth, the cloud is universal and poorly distributed. Some countries and organizations are powerfully endowed, while others are lagging. The reasons

---

[1] https://en.wikipedia.org/wiki/ARPANET

are many and never simple. From insufficient infrastructures to a non-existent legal framework, from urban legends to psychological barriers, there are as many types of reluctance as reluctant people.

Over the last decade, the cloud has been my daily life. First as the Office 365 Launch Lead for Microsoft in countries like Nigeria, Kenya and Ivory Coast. Then as sales and technical director for Microsoft in sub-Saharan Africa. And currently, as head of marketing of cloud technologies for Microsoft over the same geography. I had the chance to encounter the best and the worst, and to learn from all those experiences. To learn what works, what does not and mistakes to avoid. This book is a synthesis of those years, organized in seven steps.

The first chapter, **The cloud, this beautiful Nebula**, defines what the cloud is. It first describes what its characteristics are, its different service models, the different types of cloud and discusses the concepts of virtual machines and redundancy. It continues with the promises of the cloud and ends with a view about Africa. The latter can easily be extrapolated to other emerging markets.

In the second chapter, **Limits and constraints of the cloud**, you learn about security issues, about the need for bandwidth and the focal point of cost. It ends with a pinch of green IT and the position of the cloud under the constraints of reduction of energy consumption.

Urban legends is the title of chapter three. It addresses four major urban legends of the cloud: its lack of security, its legal limits, the potential loss of control and the ultimate Internet addiction.

Chapter four, **Legislation**, is dedicated to issues of sovereignty, protection, security, and confidentiality of personal data. It describes the legal frameworks of Europe, the United States, the Island of Mauritius and South Africa, to highlight the differences between mature and emerging markets. Finally, it addresses the issue of the protection of intellectual property and describes the challenges of responsibility. It ends with the applicable laws and the notion of contract, paramount at time of mergers and acquisitions.

There's no successful cloud deployment without the implementation of **Best practices**. It is the purpose of chapter five. Reviewing best practices avoids mistakes and accelerates the adoption of cloud technology in the organization. It also addresses new jobs created by cloud technologies.

The sixth chapter, **Chances and opportunities**, focuses on how the cloud helps organizations transform. It takes three perspectives: customer engagement, employee commitment and transformation of the organization. It is a chapter that shows how the cloud revolutionizes organizations, allowing them to reinvent themselves.

The seventh and final chapter, **And now what do we do?**, explains how to get started. After considering all aspects, technical, legal, human and organizational, here comes the time to launch the first project. How to choose it wisely, then, how to capitalize on its success to embark the whole organization in a complete transformation journey.

You will finally find in appendices, a section on virtual servers offers, comparing different providers, another one on the artificial intelligence services offerings and finally a brief introduction to the blockchain, the ultimate cloud service that will transform the world in a very profound way.

In the end, you will, hopefully, have a clearer vision of the challenges and the great benefits of the cloud. You'll be ready to start your first project or to continue your journey to more cloud.

If the cloud is now well anchored in our societies, and thanks to universal services like Uber, Airbnb or WhatsApp, a long way remains to go before organizations adapt, transform and adopt the cloud entirely. However, the movement seems inevitable. Under pressure from shareholders, customers, and employees, organizations cannot continue to spend millions of dollars in servers, networks, and private data centers. Just as the production of electricity or water, or the services of public utilities and sewage, the cloud brings these shared services that allow organizations to focus on their business and innovation. The cloud is a great catalyst for innovation.

We are only at the beginning of the fourth industrial revolution. Find out in the following pages what fuels it! Good reading.

Poitiers, France, September 5, 2017.

1.   The cloud, this beautiful Nebula

"To set man free it is enough that we help one another to realize that there does exist a goal towards which all mankind is striving. Why should we not strive towards that goal together, since it is what unites us all? The surgeon pays no heed to the moanings of his patient: beyond that pain, it is the man he is seeking to heal. That surgeon speaks a universal language. The physicist does the same when he ponders those almost divine equations in which he seizes the whole physical universe from the atom to the nebula. Even the simple shepherd modestly watching his sheep under the stars would discover, once he understood the part he was playing, that he was something more than a servant, was a sentinel. And each sentinel among men is responsible for the whole of the empire."

Wind, Sand and Stars, Antoine de St Exupéry

It is nowadays impossible to talk about computers, information systems, or applications, without talking about the cloud. The cloud is everywhere! We use it as Mr. Jourdain spoke in prose, without knowing it! It is the cloud that has enabled the explosive development of smartphones and tablets, through the "apps" and connected services.

All you need is an electronic device, an application and an Internet connection, and you are connected to this cloud computing nebula. Everything is connected nowadays: our TV, our phones, our computers obviously and more and more different objects of the house like our fridge, our hi-fi system, our light bulbs or our locks. No possible ways to escape.

And yet, if most individuals have entered the cloud era, private and public companies are still dragging their feet. The reasons are multiple and related mainly to fear and a perception of loss of control. Over the following pages, we will study these reasons and demystify them. However, perception is not reason. For a clear majority of people, skydiving is dangerous. There is, however, statistically, therefore rationally, infinitely less accident in skydiving than in car driving. The same can be said of the cloud. The reality is that despite some massive data theft cases, the public cloud is often more secure than a private data center, for the reasons I would describe in Chapter 3, Urban Legends.

The fact is that the use of the cloud is constantly increasing and there is no reason for it to stop. Before going further on its pros and cons, let's answer the first question of this book, what is the cloud?

What is the Cloud?

We talk about it so much, we end up wondering what it is. Ask ten different people, you will have ten different answers. To give the most exhaustive answer possible, I went to ask ten different internet sites. This is an anthology of answers to start on a good mood note.

Let's start with the definition of one of the major players of the cloud, a "pure player," i.e. having only cloud offer, Salesforce (http://www.salesforce.com/cloudcomputing/):

"Cloud computing is a kind of outsourcing of computer programs. Using cloud computing, users are able to access software and applications from wherever they need, while it is being hosted by an outside party — in "the cloud""

Pretty simple and straightforward definition in which it's all about having hosted applications somewhere that you can access universally.

Let's move on to Oracle, a major IT company, database, business applications and Enterprise Servers provider (https://www.oracle.com/cloud/index.html):

The Cloud "is a computing style based on shared and flexible resources, offered to users in free access, in a gradual way and using web technologies."

There are other important concepts here. The resources are shared, much like an airliner, you don't own it, but you use it when you need it. It is accessed gradually, which means according to needs one can access to a little or a lot of the power of these resources. We will come back to this "elasticity" of access.

Ask Microsoft, through its technical director for France, Bernard Ourghanlian (http://lexpansion.lexpress.fr/high-tech/le-cloud-computing-explique-aux-nuls_1384009.html), translated from the French:

"Cloud computing is accessing computer resources that are somewhere, through the Internet."

I like "somewhere"! Because, as we will see later, knowing where data and applications are can have important implications in terms not only of speed and latency (an important concept we will see later) but also regarding legal protection and data access.

Now let's ask the gigantic free online encyclopedia Wikipedia (https://en.wikipedia.org/wiki/Cloud_computing) :

"Cloud computing is an information technology paradigm that enables ubiquitous access to shared pools of configurable system resources and higher-level services that can be rapidly provisioned with minimal management effort, often over the Internet."

We introduce the concepts of configurable system resources. Because in the end, it is a question of accessing computers that will allow us to perform certain operations, such as, for example, access to e-mails, book an airplane ticket or backup documents.

Let's end with the definition considered official of the *National Institute of Standards and Technology*, in the special publication 800-145 (http://nvlpubs.nist.gov/nistpubs/Legacy/SP/nistspecialpublication800-145.pdf) :

"Cloud Computing is a model for enabling ubiquitous, convenient, on-demand network access to a shared pool of configurable computing resources (e.g., networks, servers, storage, applications, and services) that can be rapidly provisioned and released with minimal management effort or service provider interaction. This cloud model is composed of five essential characteristics, three service models, and four deployment models."

The less than one can say is that this definition seems to be more accurate than those provided by the big software houses. This is not surprising from the body that defines the standards. There is, however, a new important aspect that was not indicated in the previous definitions, namely the minimal interaction with the service provider. Indeed, the very notion of cloud computing is to be able to dispose of applications, services or storage automatically through an Internet portal, without interaction of a human operator. However, we will see that the human component is important when it comes to taking advantage of the power of the cloud. In fact, if access to services can be fully automated, the application of its services to our needs often requires a lot of reflection and sweat.

Let's summarize before going deeper into the features, service and deployment models that are critical to understanding cloud computing challenges. The cloud is about, first, using Internet technologies (networks, applications). It is then that of shared servers allowing to perform various IT operations according to its needs, in a fast and most automated possible way, without owning anything but an internet connection. Still, the latter is not usually owned, but rented.

Here are few examples of using the cloud for a simple approach to the posed problem.

Email

This is often one of the first cloud services used by individuals and businesses. Mailboxes are located somewhere in a data center and are accessible from all types of hardware, phones, tablets, and computers. Any Gmail, Hotmail (now Outlook.com) or Yahoo user has her mailbox in a data center managed by, respectively, Google, Microsoft or Oath.

More and more companies are renting the services of Google, Microsoft or other providers to manage their e-mail services. If they are based on the same software as the consumer services, they are differentiated by increased security, the use of custom domain names and guaranteed uptime. We will go into detail on these important characteristics of the quality of service.

Document sharing

Document sharing is the service that made Dropbox famous, as well as services like Flickr or OneDrive. One of the challenges with email is the technical inability to send "big" files. Imagine having to share your holiday photos with your friends or project-related documents by sending them by email.

Two major problems: first, e-mail can limit the size of attachments limiting *de facto* sending these documents. Then if you can send such a mail, it will create copies of your documents. Worse! If you send ten documents to five recipients, each of these people will receive a copy of these ten documents in his mailbox. If these documents are due to be modified, you may soon end up with several versions of the same document, all circulating by email. A challenge that often turns into a nightmare.

By using a document-sharing service, each recipient receives a link to the documents and accesses them, depending on the user rights set by the owner of those documents. It is also possible to automatically replicate the shared documents on our computer so that they can be used even without an Internet connection. This replication takes place most often in the background, without the user being aware of it.

The customer relationship management

Salesforce.com understood that the best place to aggregate the customer's data was the cloud. Any company that has customers and a salesforce to manage them is more and more using a customer relationship management software, the famous CRM. Any company that has implemented a CRM knows the pain that it can represent. Financial pain first, as it requires a lot of hardware, software and personalization service. Organizational pain then, as it often needs a review of its internal processes. The human pain finally because if there is one thing that all the salespersons of the world share is the horror of administrative tasks and a CRM is often considered a cumbersome obligation.

A CRM in the cloud eliminates financial pain and mitigates the other two because of the flexibility and modernity involved. Flexibility since it can be used everywhere on any type of devices. Even on the move, the seller has access to all her customers' data, a positively perceived feature.

Often billed by the customer or user, the return on investment is immediately quantifiable. Finally, and I will come back to this point in more detail later, the direct beneficiary being the sales department, the latter can partially free itself from the IT department to implement a CRM in the cloud. The lack of necessary hardware and software makes it possible for the department to place the order directly. With all the pros and cons attached to it, as we will see a little further.

Archiving and Backup

Another commonly-subscribed service is archiving and backup. Storage of data in the cloud is generally redundant, often in the form of RAID 1 or 5, therefore carrying a risk of loss much lower than that of a tape, for a fraction of the cost.

Beyond the cost of backup units and cassettes, their conservation and management can represent significant sums. Some regulated industries, such as insurance, must be able to keep data for decades. This requires significant investments in storage and its management.

This is not to mention workstations backup. With automatic data archiving, no more headaches for the IT department. Let's not forget the induced advantage when changing the PC of a user who can rely on automatic replication to find documents and configuration in minutes.

Web Services of all kinds

Of course, most Internet sites are installed in cloud data centers. Both to ensure their safety and support increased workloads during peak hours, and to be able to leverage any of the countless existing services.

For example, accessing chatbots, conversational robots that can provide first level support to users. Or adding a service of automatic translation, allowing the site to be offered in the user's self-detected language.

But the cloud also allows access to the computing power available through thousands of networked servers, to do complex mathematical calculations without the need to acquire a supercomputer. We can aggregate and store millions of terabytes of data from the flows of social networks, for instance, to carry sentiment analysis. You can also benefit from machine learning mechanisms to detect fraud or suspicious behaviors. Finally, it's possible to receive the data from connected objects (Internet of Things, IoT) to get real-time analysis.

New use cases appear every day, with the goal to provide almost unlimited resources for a fraction of the cost of their acquisition and management. Now that you have an idea (very small for the moment, because the field is infinitely vast), let's go back to what defines the cloud.

Characteristics of the Cloud

The National Institute of American Standards and Technology (NIST) has identified five key features, indicated in Figure 1-1.

Figure 1-1 - Characteristics of the cloud model

Let's look in more detail at these five characteristics that define if a data center obeys the cloud model.

On-demand self-service

Each of the services offered by the data center is available 24x7, without any human intervention. It is, therefore, possible for a user to provision a new server, to access a service or change the parameters of a database instance, without calling a human operator.

There must, therefore, be a management interface that allows all the necessary operations for the creation, the modification and the management of data Center computing environments. It should be possible to access this interface in a universal way, this is the second characteristic.

Universal access

It is possible to access the services and their management interfaces from standard network mechanisms and a variety of clients available from heterogeneous devices (Internet browsers, phones, tablets or computers). Access is usually based on the TCP/IP protocol through secure connections. Although security is not an initial characteristic of the cloud, the generalization of the use of services has dramatically increased attack surfaces, therefore secure access and usage have become an integral part of cloud base services.

Resource Pooling

IT resources, processors, storage, network, memory, are made available to users and assigned automatically according to the needs. At any given instant, it is almost impossible to know which machine provides the service since the pool manager continually optimize usage.

Cloud datacenters are called multi-tenant because their resources are shared by all users who have access to it. We will see that even in the concept of private cloud, the data center is generally multi-tenant because serving several departments within the same company.

The notion of resource pooling typically extends beyond a single data center. In fact, large providers have several locations in separate geographical areas to guarantee redundancy, and to satisfy proximity or jurisdiction needs, in order to satisfy a larger set of users. Thus, for sovereignty questions, some states do not allow the storage of "sensitive data" outside the borders of the state. This pushes providers to set up data centers in these countries. We will see in

Chapter 4, Legislation, that this can influence the storage of data and the use of certain services.

There is consequently a certain independence of the location, the user not fully knowing where his data or the machine that serves his request is. However, it is sometimes possible to choose a region, a country, or even a data center according to one's constraints and needs. For example, a German company may require that its data be stored in German territory. A provider who would not have a data center on German territory would then not be able to service this client.

Elasticity

Elasticity is the ability to allocate resources from the available pool (see previous features) depending on the demand and releasing them when the demand is less strong. Like a rubber that you can stretch and that will get back to its initial size when the applied force decreases.

The Figure 1-2 shows us several examples of elasticity to respond to requests for which load prediction is difficult, if not impossible, in the case of for instance of increasing use of systems in case of greater success than expectations.

Figure 1-2 - Elasticity of the Cloud model

Elasticity avoids the acquisition of computer capacity necessary to satisfy peak loads, but unused most of the time. Elasticity also applies to individual components. It is possible for example to need more computational capacity at a specific time, without the network resources being impacted. The opposite is also possible. The size of the data center allows the application to be modulated in an elastic way without the user being penalized by a bottleneck.

Measured Service

Any service usage is measured to be able to charge it, or at a minimum to provide a detailed report. This allows paying only what one uses and calculate the return on investment of the consumed resources. All this, without the need to consider the depreciation of the equipment or its maintenance, since there is no acquisition. A bit like a car rental that offers you a time and several kilometers for a specific price without the need to acquire the vehicle, to purchase insurance and to service it.

Most cloud vendors provide accurate resource utilization reports, including at granular levels. HDInsight Services at Microsoft, for example, can be billed per minute, while a virtual machine can be rented for a month, whether you are using it or not. The important thing is to be able to provide accurate reports to administrators to optimize their uses.

Service Models: IaaS, PaaS, SaaS

The service model defines what you are managing and what the cloud provider provides. The NIST defines three service models:

1. Infrastructure as a Service or IaaS.
2. Platform as a Service or PaaS.
3. Application as a Service or SaaS.

You will find in the literature reference to other service models, such as Data as a Service or DaaS. These are just submodels of the above three, usually used for marketing purpose or to highlight a service offered by a provider.

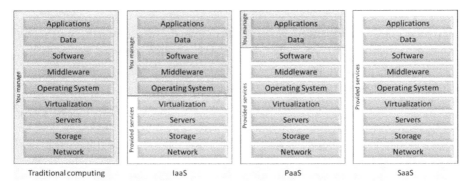

Figure 1-3 - Service Models

To fully understand the three service models, we need to look at the operation of a server that provides a service to a client. Between the network connector and the application exposed to the user, there is a set of hardware and services, illustrated in Figure 1-3. Adapted from the model of OSI Communication (*Open System Interconnection*), you may find some variations, but the main idea remains the same.

If you start from the end user running an application (the top of the diagram), the latter will require access to data. Application and data are often implemented from a software brick and a middleware that abstracts the operating system. This is what will allow the use of the same application on several different operating systems, such as Windows Server and Linux Red Hat. The operating system usually works in a virtual machine, allowing to run several "logical servers" within a single "physical server". Virtualization has been mainstream for several years with the increase of the available computing power of the servers. It makes it easier to take advantage of the server's resources and provides greater flexibility to separate workloads. The physical server is finally connected to a disk array, increasingly in SSD form (*Solid State Drive*) for performance and reliability issues and connected to a network to access it.

With this diagram in mind, we can now more easily explain the three service models.

Infrastructure as a Service

The Infrastructure as a Service is the availability of virtual servers, as shown in Figure 1-3. The user then has access to the virtualization platform to create his own virtual machines and to install the operating system of his choice.

Usually, the service provider will allow to customize the type of machine or even to choose pre-configured machines. For example, at the date of writing this book, Microsoft offers Linux machines (Ubuntu, Red Hat, Suse, and R), as well as Windows Server machines (raw, Biztalk, Java, SharePoint, and SQL).

I will come back to the types of servers proposed by the major providers to better understand the stakes in the part Choosing your virtual machine.

The important point to understand is that in the Infrastructure as a Service model, the virtual machine administrator is fully responsible for it. He can install what he wants on this server, configure it as he likes, guarantee its security, patch it and update it constantly. He must also setup redundancy if necessary. The shutdown, unintentional or not, of the physical server, causes the virtual servers shutdown. Therefore, it's not because the data center is redundant that, by default, your virtual machine is. You need to take this into account when creating a new virtual machine. Remember that except for the hardware, with an Infrastructure as a Service, you are in charge of everything else.

Platform as a Service

The Platform as a Service allows you to install the software of your choice on an operating system already configured. For example, you want to implement a SharePoint site or an ERP without having to worry about the underlying machines, welcome to PaaS.

If the latter offers total flexibility in terms of the configuration of the applications you are running, you will also have to manage it in terms of updates, backup, or load increase. On the other hand, you do not worry about the underlying platform. No need to update the operating system and its various services, these are managed by the provider.

The PaaS model is particularly well suited to administrators who need application flexibility and want to get rid of hardware management. Requiring less work than the SaaS model, it offers a granular control of the application.

A service on the edge of the PaaS and SaaS models is the one proposed by the containers, of which Docker is a flagship provider. Without going into the details of the containers, they allow, on Linux systems, to package an application and its dependencies in an isolated environment that can be run on any Linux server. Thus, it is possible to "move" an application from one platform to another, from a private cloud to a public cloud for example.

Software as a Service

It's probably with the Software as a Service model that we find the biggest choice of services. It's not just a matter of choosing a type of virtual machine or a software platform, but of executing a service, whatever it may be. Most applications running on a smartphone or tablet today use the software as a service model. When you use Facebook, you are in a SaaS, probably without realizing it.

The first service that comes to mind is usually messaging. It is the fastest growing service, along with social networks. When you check your e-mail messages, whether on Gmail, Yahoo!, or outlook.com, you connect to a mail server that manages your mailbox. If you use an Internet Explorer to view your messages, you first use a web server that itself will connect to the mail server. In fact, you then use two services: the one that manages the display of pages in your browser and the one that manages your messages.

Over time, the number and type of services offered by cloud service providers exploded. From instant messaging to backup, from business intelligence to predictive analysis, from multifactor authentication to multimedia services, the offer is colossal.

The main advantage of the SaaS model is usually its speed of implementation. No need for expensive hardware or software. Choose the service, subscribe, start it and in a few minutes, hours or days, you get your first results. All for a fraction of the cost of an on-premises solution.

The downside is that you totally outsource those services to a provider who can decide overnight to stop the service or transform it drastically, forcing you to change strategy. However, this mode evolves very quickly and even an on-premises solution can be subject to the same hazards.

SaaS's demand has exploded in recent years because of its excellent return on investment ratios. In fact, it is now possible to access services that were once reserved for very large organizations because of their exorbitant costs of operation. With service pooling, these costs have fallen dramatically. For example, it is now possible to do predictive analysis for a few tens of euros per month, with services proposed by Google, Amazon, or Microsoft. This will help to implement business strategies, measuring impact and adapting to demand.

Now that we have defined the cloud models, let us have a look at the different types of clouds.

Types of Cloud

The NIST defines four types of cloud, also known as deployment models: private, community, hybrid and public. For questions of simplification, I do not distinguish between the private and community cloud. The reason is simple: the private cloud is limited to an organization, the community cloud to a set of organizations whose needs are generally shared, who know each other and have no confidence challenges. Let's look at their features.

Private Cloud

The private cloud is, as its name implies, reserved for a single organization. The question then arises as to the difference between a data center (or a technical room) and a private cloud. The answer should simply be looked at by the characteristics of the data center. If the five characteristics of the cloud apply, it is a private cloud. If not, it is just a data center.

What difference does it really make? Substantial! It concerns the management and the use of resources. A data center constrained by limitations in personnel or hardware cannot claim to be a private cloud and therefore the advantages that are associated with it. It may seem anecdotal, but it is not, because it depends on who holds the power.

In the case of a traditional data center, power is in the hands of the one who exploits it. In the case of a private cloud, it is in the hands of the one who uses it. Certainly, whoever exploits it may decide to stop or change its operation, but that would go against its service contract. From the moment there is a service contract, the power goes into the hands of the user. And that is, in my opinion, what makes the difference between the traditional data center and private cloud.

The distinction is even more important when you want to implement a hybrid cloud strategy, you should start by analyzing your own environment. Charity begins at home! Without the private cloud, no hybrid cloud is possible. Once again this may seem anecdotal, but the many painful experiences of implementing hybrid cloud have told me that everything always begins by applying to oneself the characteristics of the cloud before wanting to move on to the next step.

And what is this step?

Hybrid Cloud

The hybrid cloud is based on the best of both worlds: implementing a private cloud and moving some workloads to a public cloud while administering all services in a homogeneous way.

So, what are the benefits? The first one is flexibility. You use a public infrastructure, platform, or services when your infrastructure, platform, or private services do not allow the implementation of what you need. For example, you can choose to migrate your mail to a public cloud while maintaining your file server services in your private cloud.

The second interest is growth. You may find yourself constrained by your private infrastructure while needing more computing, storage or services that you do not have locally, to meet users demand. Instead of making a ruckus or waiting weeks or months for the necessary capacity, a public cloud can offer you the solution.

Now if on paper the hybrid cloud seems an ideal solution, it's not always easy to implement. Many questions will quickly arise, starting with authentication and security, continuing with the management of all services. It is always possible to tinker, but to implement a professional solution, transparent to the end user is often more complex than it seems. It is therefore important to take the time to make a complete tour of the user experience and to accept no compromise on security, not risking introducing potential flaws in your system.

What about the public cloud?

Public Cloud

The public cloud is usually the one referred to by default when the word "cloud" is used. The data center that provides public cloud services is generally located far from the end user, sometimes in unknown and very remote locations.

One of the main features of a public cloud is it is shared by a large number of users. We are talking about "multi-tenant", that is, a hardware and software infrastructure shared by all users.

There are "software barriers" between each of the public cloud users so that Mr. X does not have access to the data of Madame Y, but the entire hardware environment (and this goes well beyond the servers or network infrastructure) is fully managed by the service provider. The service guarantee is then paramount.

Before exploring the myths and realities of the cloud, be it public, private or hybrid, let us pause for a moment on the notion of the virtual machine and its choice. After many discussions, it appears that many users and administrators have a fairly limited view on servers. However, not all servers are alike and depending on their needs, you should choose the server best suited to the service you want to run.

Choosing your virtual machine

Before choosing a server, you should ask yourself a number of questions about its computing power, memory, interfaces and optimization, all based on its usage. The rule also applies to the choice of a virtual machine in a public cloud.

Amazon calls its environment EC2 (for *Elastic Compute Cloud*), Google simply Compute Engine, Orange Business Flexible Computing Services, and Microsoft or Gandi.net is only talking about virtual machines. Most providers typically offer preconfigured machine offers that meet a particular type of operations.

In fact, depending on the needs, this or that server is better suited. A bit like choosing a vehicle to move houses, between a pickup truck and a forty-foot container, the offer is vast and suitable for volume and distance. The same is applicable to servers. Generally, offers are structured around five major types of uses:

1. *General Purpose Machine*. This is the entry-level option for a general-purpose machine balanced in terms of computing power, memory and storage. This type of server is chosen for database applications, collaborative servers, or messaging. You choose the number of cores and the memory size depending on the number of users or simultaneous requests, or the size of the data.
2. *Machine Optimized for calculation*. These are machines that offer a large computing power with faster and more processors. We're going

to turn to these servers for high-traffic websites, massively parallel game platforms, video encoding or scientific calculus.

3. *Machine Optimized for memory*. The typical server with a large memory for processing requiring a large amount of data. These are the ideal machines for Big data, data processing in the context of a data warehouse, ERP like SAP with SAP Hana, or website caching to improve rendering.

4. *Machine optimized for video processing*. A powerful GPU (*Graphics Processing Unit*) is at the heart of these machines. If you need to make 3D rendering calculations, encode videos in real time, or generate videos for fluid mechanics, for example, these machines are an ideal choice.

5. *Optimized Machine for high performance*. In the same vein as those optimized for calculation, we move on to the next step to get into the world of supercomputers (HPC, *High-Performance Computing*). This is the world of massively parallel machines with very high-speed network interfaces. It includes the calculations of fluid mechanics, seismic or oil research, risk calculation, weather forecasting, molecular modeling or genomics, in short everything that requires a huge computational power.

Some providers, such as Google, simplify this approach by limiting their pre-packaged offers and proposing options. Others, like Microsoft or Amazon, have a catalog of pre-packaged offers worthy of a very long restaurant menu in which it is not easy to circulate. Whatever choice you make, you should always start with a pilot or proof of concept. Rates range from a few cents an hour to hundreds of dollars depending on the machine. Forgetting to unplug a virtual machine can become very costly. I will deepen the right approach in chapter 5, Best practices.

> **Note** You will find in the appendix a non-exhaustive list of the server offers of the major cloud providers.

Data centers, cloud, redundancy and "Tier"

There is another related topic to the type of cloud that is the notion of « Tier ». I met a lot of customers who insisted on the "level" of their data center or their provider's. Let us be clear, this level defines only one characteristic of the data center: the availability of its infrastructure. At no point does the tier goes down at the server or software level. It can, therefore, be said that the Tier is necessary for evaluating the quality of the data center, but in no case sufficient.

There are two classifications of that level of availability:

- One that is a standard defined by the Telecommunications Industry Association (TIA) Accredited by the American Standards Institute (ANSI), ANSI/TIA-942. Called the Data Center Standards Overview, this standard describes the specifications for a data center.
- Another one that has been designed and defined by a private service company, the Uptime Institute (https://uptimeinstitute.com).

If the two classifications define four levels of availability of a data center, the first is an official standard, the second is purely private. They both define the precise characteristics of a data center's infrastructure, from wiring to power to air conditioning. These four levels are as follows:

1. Tier 1. No redundancy of the components. Failure of one of the components, such as a UPS, can result in the failure of the entire data center and therefore stop the service to its customers. The expected availability is 99.671% or 28.8 hours maximum downtime per year. It should be noted that if this first level does not define any redundancy, it does, however, define a minimum protection of the electrical distribution in the form of inverters and generators in case of shutdown of the electrical distribution, and cooling (air or any other cooling mechanism of the computer components) of the data center.
2. Tier 2. The specifications of Tier 1 to which the redundancy of the electrical distribution and cooling of the data center is added. This means that the inverters are redundant, as well as the generators and the air conditioning system. However, only one distribution path is in place. The expected availability is 99.741% or 22.7 hours maximum downtime per year.
3. Tier 3. The Tier 2 specifications to which the distribution path redundancy is added, with only one being active at a time. This means that any of the components can be stopped for maintenance without

the customer service being affected. The expected availability is 99.982% or 1.58 hours maximum downtime per year.

4. Tier 4. The Tier 3 specifications to which the automated fault tolerance is added. If one of the components fails, the second service distribution network takes over without human intervention. The expected availability is 99.995% or 26.28 minutes of maximum downtime per year.

Again, a big exclamation point should be blinking in front of your eyes! The availability defined by the TIA 942 Standard or the Uptime Institute is only applicable to the data center infrastructure. In the event of a major software outage, such as massive corruption by a virus, the actual availability of access to the service may fall apart, while that of the infrastructure is in no way impacted.

Finally, these levels do not define the quality or redundancy of the server components. It is, therefore, possible in theory to have a Tier 4 datacenter with servers with no redundancy, no duplicate network card, no Raid 1 disks, no clusters, etc. It seems very important to have a good discussion with the service provider to understand how much redundancy is in place. Indeed, marketing tends to suggest that everything is redundant, but the reality is sometimes different and the notion of Tier, or rather ignorance of its meaning, tends to obscure this reality. I've met many furious customers, having suffered web servers downtime, believing, wrongly, that the virtual servers that were running them were totally redundant.

The promises of the cloud, myth or reality?

So, what about the promises of the cloud? The latter is the long-awaited Grail: the end of the supreme reign of computer scientists and the beginning of the power of the users? If this part may not be exhaustive, it looks at the cloud through five lenses: control, security, flexibility, performance, and costs.

Control, loss or gain?

The first cloud-related myth is the loss of control, and thus implicitly the loss of the power of the IT department (and potential loss of jobs).

The first idea is that by moving a local server service to a public cloud, the management of the hardware and potentially the software on which the service in question is based is effectively eliminated. If we extrapolate to all the hardware and software, it appears that the person who took care of this management become unnecessary. But is it totally true? Let's take an example in the three cloud models:

- IaaS. We move one or more virtual machines (VM) from the local data center to a public cloud. Which VM to choose? How to integrate it into the existing environment? How do you ensure security, redundancy or backup? Here are a few questions to ask. Certainly, if you have a technician or a service provider that is devoted to the preparation and configuration of the equipment, you will have to consider what that person will do. It is very likely that you need to reconfigure your team to abandon the management of the equipment, manage VMs and integrate them into your private cloud. It should be noted that the current trend is moving towards the hybrid cloud. This creates new development opportunities for personnel in charge of the existing data center hardware.

- PaaS. I would be tempted to say that nothing changes, or so little. In fact, managing a database server in your data center or on the other side of the planet does not have an honest impact on the day-to-day tasks. It is necessary to install the appropriate software, to manage its operation and its data, and possibly to see with the team in charge of the equipment to adapt the latter to increasing needs.

- SaaS. Local or remote mail administrator, to take an example, both have the same duties. On the other hand, the opportunities to extend his power are huge. In an environment constrained by the infrastructure or the platform, it is necessary to constantly arbitrate. While in an open and flexible environment, the cloud offers endless choices! Certainly, all the options available in private cloud may not be accessible, but it is for the benefits of an infinity of new options.

What about the final loss of control? A real myth! The only control that is lost is the one on the purchase and maintenance of the equipment. For the rest of the tasks, you continue to have the hand, a hundred percent.

Now, let's face it. In terms of value added, the choice of hardware, its acquisition, and its maintenance are relatively small tasks. To take a simple parallel, imagine having to manage a fleet of company cars. It is very likely that a dealership will be better equipped with equipment and personnel to manage purchase, maintenance and routine servicing than a garage you would manage in the company. Do you lose control over your fleet? Or asking differently: Do you need hardware control and maintenance of your fleet? It is very likely that the answer is negative. It is the same with the alleged loss of control of your server set.

It is clear, however, through the previous examples that a category of staff will be faced with two choices: changing missions or leaving the company. This decision is not to be taken lightly, but it generally induces an increase in the interest of the missions. Any change can be painfully experienced, and I will detail the required change management to be considered in chapter 5, Best Practices.

Security, loss or gain?
Security is a complex subject that I deal with in detail in Chapter 2, Limitations and constraints of the cloud. But let's look at the impact on the security of a cloud environment.

Since the exponential usage increase of the Internet and the applications that support it, threats have continued to rise along with the surfaces exposed to these threats, which generally increases the vulnerability of systems. By taking security measures, the risks are reduced without ever being able to cancel them. The only way to totally secure a system is to make it totally hermetic to external influences, which has little interest, unless you want to make it a completely closed network, like some networks that exist in research or defense projects, which are out of the scope of this book.

IT security is precisely defined through the suite of standards ISO/IEC 27000. This suite contains all the information security standards published by the International Standards Organization (ISO) and the International Electrotechnical Commission (CIE) under the name " Information Technology — Security Techniques ». It's not my purpose to dissect these standards (several thousands of pages, if you want, you can start here: https://www.iso.org/obp/ui#iso:std:iso-iec:27000:ed-3:v1:en). However, it is most likely that you have not submitted your own data center to the yardstick of the suite of the standards ISO/IEC 27000, starting with ISO/IEC 27001.

What does this mean for your information? Here is a summary that I hope simple. ISO/IEC 27001 describes the setup of an Information Security Management System (ISMS), the basis for securing any information system. If your data center follows the principles and implements one of the one hundred and fourteen good practices described in ISO/IEC 27002, then there is a strong bet that your data is highly secure. If not, which concerns a vast majority of companies in both Africa and the rest of the world, there are one or more flaws potentially exploitable by external or internal threats.

Conversely, all serious public cloud providers comply with minimum ISO/IEC 27001:

- Microsoft: https://www.microsoft.com/en-us/trustcenter/compliance/complianceofferings
- Amazon: https://aws.amazon.com/compliance/iso-27001-faqs/
- Google: https://support.google.com/work/answer/6056694
- Salesforce: http://content.trust.salesforce.com/trust/en/learn/compliance/
- Ovh: https://www.ovh.com/us/about-us/certifications.xml

Generally, these same providers comply with the ISO/IEC 27017 and 27018 standards, which are specific to public clouds and which are, respectively, a complimentary guide to good practices defined by the 27002 standards and a practical guide to the protection of personal data (also known as personal identification information, PII).

It appears clearly, with a closer look, that data stored by a provider complying with ISO/IEC 27000 standards are safer than in a computer system that does not respect it. Safety wise, it is an obvious gain.

Generally, depending on the industries and countries, other specific standards can be added. This is, for example, the case of the "European Union Model Clauses" or the "*The Esquema Nacional de Seguridad*". Again, this is an additional guarantee of compliance with industry or state rules.

Flexibility, loss or gain?

Let's say your company decides to launch a new product or service. The latter requires a digital infrastructure to work. This can be a new application, the extension or the addition of a new application module. In any case, you will need a complex underlying infrastructure.

And here you go again: acquisition of new hardware, negotiation of budgets and preparation of the environment to cater for this new system. Unfortunately for your company, the new product is not up to expectations and the decision is made to stop it. Here you are with useless available computing power, if not totally unusable because very specialized.

Now let's imagine that your choice goes to a cloud solution. You have been able to evolve your needs as the new product is marketed, increasing or diminishing the needed capacity. When the decision to unplug occurs, you can simply free servers and services with a single click.

The flexibility of the services offered by cloud providers can also be studied. Beyond the new production system goes its development and testing, its load increase and its management. Creating a test platform in the cloud does not require any heavy investment and has no impact on the production systems. It is then possible to have a completely isolated environment with which one can carry out all possible and imaginable tests without taking any risks. A huge benefit especially when you don't want to risk and immobilize large sums.

You may also want to start small, "to test the water". Installing it in a public cloud allows you to be able to meet any need for a brutal increase in workload, avoiding a performance drop and potentially dissatisfaction of users.

So, for flexibility, the gain is noticeable, almost from the first minute of use.

Performance, loss or gain?

With security, performance is one of the most controversial topics. First, performance is both measurable, therefore objective, and perceived, therefore subjective. Second, the pure performance of an application or process is often the result of a set of interdependent components. Finally, even if you imagine being able to isolate the performance of an application to a single server, you can see by looking at Figure 1-3 - Service Models, that each of the layers has an impact on the objective performance of the application.

Let's take a simple example. Let's say you're hosting a file server in your data center. Each user stores the information he or she needs to do his or her daily work. The performance of access to each of these files is limited by the speed of the network, the hard disks on which the files are stored, and the processor power that must interpret and service each access request. So, we can imagine that if a very large number of users want to access their files at the same time, the server, the disks, and the network will be used, and the access times will increase.

With the growth of the files, you quickly get to saturation of your storage arrays. It is then necessary to find a solution beyond just adding new hard drives. You then decide to store your users' files in the cloud. And there, the performance is collapsing because if your storage and the power of the servers have increased dramatically, it is not your network that becomes a bottleneck. You decide that the performance of the cloud is not up to your expectations.

Let's say that you have a data-intensive application that your users have access to in client-server mode. Only relatively small result sets are served to the clients. On the other hand, obtaining these results requires a large volume of data and a high computational power. As the data grows and users' requests get more complex, performances will be reduced. You then decide to migrate the application to the cloud, taking care to setup multiple virtual machines to serve user requests. In a few days, users smile again, their requests returning their results almost instantly. You have leveraged the computing power of virtual servers designed for speed and virtually unlimited fast storage, which would have been impossible on-premises without massive investment.

I could take many more examples, but I think you have understood the main constraint we have encountered: performance relies on your applications and services architecture. That's why many users are disappointed with the unfulfilled promise of cloud performance. Without prior thinking, you risk disappointment. However, by putting a little of analytical effort, performance gains can be exponential.

Costs, loss or gain?

Well, let's demystify the question of cost from the get-go. If you choose the cloud to save money, chances are you will be immensely disappointed and disillusioned. Not that the cloud is more expensive than a local solution, but it is worth looking at the total cost of acquiring and operating the solution to be able to derive an increase or a decrease in price.

Often the confusion comes from the fact that for a given workload, the infrastructure, the servers and the software are sometimes already there. In addition, components such as electricity, air conditioning, required real estate or operating personnel are variable. Those are costs that do not always appear on the IT department's financial balance sheet. Then, when it comes to subscribing to a cloud service and we compare cloud prices with those of acquiring or renting a locally installed software solution, many administrators choke and find the pricing scandalous.

Therefore, evaluating the cost of a solution hosted in the cloud or on premises is not a simple game. A bit like trying to compare the costs of several telephone providers. Each coming with different offers and calculation methodology, it becomes difficult or impossible to differentiate them on a pure pricing aspect.

If the cost is a significant aspect, a Gartner survey carried in 2014 (https://www.gartner.com/doc/2643016/taming-digital-dragon-cio-agenda) teaches us that only fourteen percent of organizations use the cloud for cost benefits. However, if you are part of the fourteen percent, here are some simple tips for evaluating the cost of the cloud and comparing it to an on-premises equivalent solution.

1. *Compare the comparable*. The offers of cloud providers are generally predefined for pricing simplification. If you used to have 1-GB mailboxes and that's enough, compare the cost of this storage with the one proposed by the provider, even and especially if the proposed storage is ten or one hundred times more important. The same goes for a virtual server or any other component.
2. *Take all costs into consideration, including hidden costs*. And yes, electricity has a cost, real estate, and air conditioning too. Get closer to your finance department to evaluate all the costs associated with a computer solution. Don't just be limited to computer hardware and

software. Consider the integration and increased bandwidth requirements. Finally, do not forget maintenance, software, hardware and human costs.

3. *Discuss in-depth acquisition (and therefore amortization) and renting with an accountant*. All public cloud providers will explain to you that operational expenditures (OpEx) are preferable to capital expenditures (CapEx), as this suits them well. If at first glance this seems preferable during time of financial scarcity, during which investments decrease, it depends on many factors that only your CFO will be able to help you evaluate objectively relatively to the goals of the company.

4. *Consider the costs in the long term*. It is important to evaluate the operating time of the solution to calculate the actual cost.

5. *Make a return on investment analysis*. More and more IT departments act as profit centers. It is, therefore, easier for them to calculate the potential return on investment of a solution. The cloud typically allows this type of analysis more quickly than an on-premises solution due to pricing simplification. This is also a good way to convince the financiers to spend some money.

As a rule, the notion of cost sharing plays in favor of the cloud, but do not let yourself be abused. It is sometimes better to continue using a depreciated material based on an existing infrastructure, rather than revolutionize everything. In addition, change management can induce extra costs depreciable over many years. Sometimes the *Status Quo* Is preferable to the revolution, especially when it comes to spending money that the company has had so much trouble earning. So for the costs, it's a draw.

Conclusion

So, let's summarize the situation on the five axes defined beforehand: control, security, flexibility, performance, and costs.

We find out that on three dimensions out of five the cloud is beneficial, this is not clear on the other two. This rather a tie. So, depending on the weight of each of those dimensions, you will be more able to make a rational decision to go or not to the cloud.

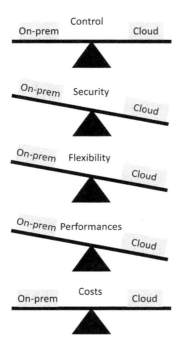

Figure 1-4 - Control, security, flexibility, performance, and costs

Now, on the African continent, is there another reading grid, or does the situation on the continent affect whether to go to the cloud? Let's look at this in detail.

The situation in Africa

What are the main differences between the situation in Africa and that of other continents? My experience of these last years of cloud technologies sales on the African continent led me to discover the nine listed below. Beware! They are neither exhaustive nor universal and are not judgmental. These are situations that I have been confronted with and in which some readers will probably find themselves.

It is also not inevitable that the situation evolves rapidly. If we look at the quality and the price of Internet connections, they have evolved considerably over the last three years. A Skype communication was not possible three to four years ago when it is commonplace today ... in the big cities, but as soon as we move to the province areas or to the bush. the situation is still chaotic and some places remain to be covered.

1. *Customers infrastructure are poor*. I am going into detail about the state of networks in Chapter 5, Best Practices, but most companies' networks are poor. Hardware, firewall, security, directory, are usually to be audited and need to evolve before embarking on a cloud project. If not, they will experience unexpected painful complications during the implementation of any cloud project.

2. *Internet connections are expensive and limited*. It's not totally a view of the mind to say that the internet is more expensive in Africa, and in general in emerging markets, than anywhere else in the world. Admittedly, access providers will show you that no, their offers are neither more expensive nor more limited than in Europe or North America. What they omit to say is that if their position is verified to the point of entry of the country. It is quite different when it comes to reaching a server in France, Great Britain or the United States. Now, like the so-called developed countries, the quality of the connections is constantly improving and their prices falling. We also see a decrease in the dependency to VSAT at the benefit of the optical fiber or WiMax, which greatly improves speed and latency.

3. *There are no datacenters on the continent*. The fact that no public cloud data center exists on the continent[2] makes customers dependent on a very remote connection with often large latency and access times, dependent on the traffic of the country. Certainly, there are some local providers, mainly Internet access providers, but we are far from the cloud offers proposed by the major suppliers. Tier III data centers are available, i.e. offering 99.98% availability, but most are not ISO/IEC 27001 certified.

4. *The skill and understanding of the cloud are starting*. Few local computer providers have embarked on the great cloud adventure. There is a skill failure to explain what can be done and how to do it. The mountain to climb is impressive. If this is the case for large companies,

---

[2] At the time of the release of this book, IBM had a SoftLayer data center in South Africa, Microsoft had announced two datacenters in Johannesburg and Cape Town, and Amazon had announced a study of the issue.

on the other hand, many small and medium-sized businesses rely entirely on the cloud, as this allows them to have unparalleled development flexibility.

5. *The explosion of smartphones made the local web services profitable.* There are more and more companies that are created on the models of Uber, Amazon or Facebook and target local people. These startups consume a lot of cloud services, without actually ever complaining about connections or remoteness of services, demonstrating that the maturity of usage is in sharp growth.

6. *Resourcefulness is a reality.* When you don't have oil, you have ideas. Famous French slogan of the 70's, still in force on the African continent. There is always a way to get there, even if it is a little orthodox. This is the reasons sometimes a wobbly local solution is often preferred to a cloud solution.

7. *Fear of loss is often put forward.* Loss of employment due to loss of infrastructure control. Loss of sovereignty of its data because of their remoteness. Loss of computer control due to its dependence on unreliable internet connection. The impression of control by having a data center on site is still prevalent.

8. *Electricity is a real issue.* If you operate a data center, you need electrical power for your IT infrastructure and air conditioning. However, in the vast majority of African countries, electricity is of poor quality and prone to frequent cuts. As a result, data center operations are often more expensive than in Europe. It sometimes goes to the extremes, as in Nigeria for example, where each customer has its own power generator, dramatically increasing the cost of electricity.

9. *The legislation is not appropriate at best, does not exist at worst.* The development of Internet technologies has been so fast and the connection of African countries is recent, that many states have not put in place legislation to protect users, businesses or their data. In addition, a relative misunderstanding of the stakes and a confusion on risk tend to accentuate extreme positions. In fact, in the absence of an information classification policy, it is difficult to state clearly what is allowed and what is not.

So, as I indicated, all these observations do not apply everywhere, and the situation improves every day. As we are seeing in Chapter 3. Urban Legends, if these different observations are sometimes true and verified, there are also some economic solutions and therefore a change of viewpoint can result in a positive evolution of the situation with regard to cloud technologies.

However, the stakes for the continent are colossal. Some countries, such as Rwanda, Nigeria or Mauritius, to name but a few, without bias, have understood it. Having a real cloud policy, they have enabled the creation of a digital economy that brings both economic and societal development. All want their share of the Internet cake and that's the reason why we see companies like Huawei, ZTE, Microsoft, Orange or IBM investing massively. The future is digital and the billion people in Africa are not leaving the big and smaller players in the market indifferent.

2. Limitations and constraints of the cloud

« In human freedom in the philosophical sense, I am definitely a disbeliever. Everybody acts not only under external compulsion but also in accordance with inner necessity. »

As I See the World, Albert Einstein

Is the cloud the panacea, the cure for all ailments of local computing and economic development? If you cannot deny its huge contribution to the development of some companies, or even of some states, it is essential to understand its limits and constraints.

It's not to deny its qualities to look at its limits. We need to honestly accept that the cloud is not always the answer to everything and, above all, that it's neither easy nor cheap, or as fast as some providers' marketing departments paint it is. On the other hand, it is a real innovation. Properly understood, it allows organizations to go beyond the boundaries of on-premises computing and to accelerate all their ambitions of development.

We often say that sky is the limit. This generally means that there is no tangible human limit to a given topic. I tend to agree since the clouds are already there, in our terrestrial sky. The cloud carries many promises. However, some cannot be fulfilled if we do not understand our boundaries, so we can push them further.

There are three immediate limits to cloud technologies and all are on the client side. Indeed, on the provider's side, particularly with global providers like Microsoft, Amazon or Google, limits, fairly, do not exist. Their infrastructure is immense, with data centers containing millions of servers, massively redundant, geographically distributed and increasingly using renewable energy. There is almost no limit to the workloads that can be run.

The three limits and constraints on the customer's side are the following:

1. *Security*. Of applications, hardware, infrastructure, and individuals. Security-related, we find confidentiality and data sovereignty[3], essential to ensure a relative independence of states and businesses.
2. *Bandwidth*. The Internet becomes a bottleneck and potentially the weak link (*single point of failure*).
3. *Cost*. Especially the hidden financial and human costs, if we do not take the evolution of information system into consideration.

There is a fourth point in many developed countries. Its importance should grow in the months and years to come in Africa and every emerging economy: the environmental impact. Although there is no legislation in this sense in many countries as to provide incentives to use renewable energy or encourage sustainable behavior, it's very likely this will happen, and rather quickly.

Let's have a detailed look at those four topics, to infer the necessary, most economical, and most sensible process, in the short and long term.

Security

What has not been said about the Internet and its data security? While scandals are going well, from data theft at Dailymotion or Yahoo to the Panama Papers and Wikileaks, cloud security is constantly questioned. Cybercrime and

---

[3] Data sovereignty is covered in detail in Chapter 4, Legislation.

espionage are on everyone's lips. Where's the truth? Is the cloud that risky? I will consider many stories, rumors, and misconceptions in Chapter 3, Urban Legends. Let's for now look at the security of data stored in the cloud, and how to protect everything to the best of our possibilities and those offered by the service provider.

Threats

Before discussing security, let's question the threats. What are we protecting us from? Usually, the first answer that comes to mind is data theft. For an organization, this may mean intellectual property theft, theft of customer or loss of reputation. For an individual, it's access to his bank accounts, usurpation of her identity or publication of confidential information to harm the individual.

As Eric Schmidt, former CEO of Google, said: "If you have something that you don't want anyone to know, maybe you shouldn't be doing it in the first place." Easy to say, especially when it concerns genuinely confidential information which is not intended to be broadcast. Beyond the question of the storage of information, the question is: are they safer in the cloud, on a server of the company or on my personal computer? We will come back to this question.

The other threat is the destruction of information. This is the case of some viruses which merely 'just' destroy everything with the intent to harm. It is in these moments that one realizes that the backups that were made are not comprehensive or accessible. Famous Murphy's law!

Finally, in recent years, a growing threat is ransomware. This practice is either to steal data or to encrypt it and then to ask their owners a ransom to get them back or get the encryption key. This type of attack is growing from year to year. According to Kaspersky Lab, twenty percent of victims who pay do not recover their files. So, the question is: should we pay?

What do we need to do to protect ourselves from these threats? Computer security experts and publishers of security solution recommended several actions:

- **Protect yourselves**. This seems common sense, but easier said than done. While the attack surface increases (I'll come back on this notion), threats evolve constantly and user awareness lags, putting the entire system in danger.

- **Assess the risks and the costs**. Security has costs and consequences. It is not possible to protect everything unless you live in a total vacuum. The risk of data loss or theft should be assessed, and appropriate measures taken.
- **Classify information**. I dig deeper into this topic in Chapter 4, Legislation. Classifying data allows you to know what is public, what isn't, what is highly confidential and what is less. This allows implementing security rules based on the processed data.
- **Implement best practices**. Human beings are often the weakest links. Identity theft is more and more the entry point to information theft. An identity protection policy needs to be setup through strong passwords or multi-factor authentication, to limit these risks.

Basic notions of security

Information security is a broad topic. You will find many books and articles about it, as well as many companies whose unique job it is. To enjoy the safety of cloud services, it seems essential to know what we're talking about. Information security is defined by three main concepts: privacy, integrity, and availability, sometimes in addition to a fourth one: non-repudiation.

Privacy

As per ISO / IEC 27001, privacy is defined as the "right of individuals to control or influence what information related to them may be collected and stored and by whom and to whom the information may be disclosed". The identification of the users, the rights attributed to them and the encryption of information play a major role in protecting the access to information.

Integrity

Integrity means that the information is complete and accurate. This also indicates that it cannot be modified by chance, unexpectedly or maliciously. Generally, the traceability of changes, the continuous backup of previous versions and control sums are there to guaranty the information integrity.

Availability

Availability defines that access to information is available within the limits defined by its owner. In the case of the cloud, we have seen that availability was the subject of a precise classification. To this, access time may be added, which may be defined according to the type of information (data archived may require more time to be retrieved for instance than "live" data).

Non-repudiation

This is a legal feature, generally a subset of integrity. It means that the sender and receiver of information are who they claim to be and that the information sent is consistent with the information received, and has thus not been altered. The mechanism of digital certificates is generally used and accepted by justice to prove non-repudiation. You must be able to guarantee security (integrity, confidentiality, and availability) of its private key. This is where logical mechanisms as smart cards play a major role.

What about my datacenter in all this?

Now that we have defined the basic concepts and have a sense of the threats that target our information, let's see what the security of the data center is. If we want to protect our information and ensure maximum security, it must first look at the attack surface of our system.

The Attack Surface

The attack surface of a computer system can be defined by the collection of all points of entry and points of communication with the outside world. On any accessible system, it is generally important and must be precisely known. There are generally four types of attack surface:

1. The network attack surface: open ports on routers and firewalls, IP public addresses, used and available network protocols...
2. The software attack surface: entry form, operating system, services on the servers, administration interfaces...
3. The human attack surface: the reaction of the user to all solicitations that require an answer, by clicking on a link, opening an attachment or clicking on a button. Phishing or social engineering requires these actions, for instance.

4. The physical attack surface: do not forget that a data center is primarily a physical place and physical theft of data is not to be overlooked. Is physical access to the system restricted, as well as the use of hardware like USB or DVD? It is also noted that according to the McAfee[4] company more than 40 percent of data theft is still done by physical means.

It is accepted that the bigger the attack surface, the bigger the risk. One of the accountabilities of your Security Department should be to reduce this surface to a minimum. It is essential to draw up a precise mapping of this attack surface to protect all points of entry.

An article from Microsoft[5] sheds some light on the attack surface and the ways of reducing it. A point that seems important concerns what is behind an entry point. Indeed, an open port, for instance, can sometimes be useful. Behind this port, we may find services like web servers or applications like WordPress or SharePoint. Each page of these applications can be an entry point for a code injection. A detailed understanding of each of these points of entry and their potential vulnerabilities is crucial.

The concept of "defense in depth" becomes sensible. Indeed, why protecting the physical and logical perimeter of the data center, if the applications that are running inside are not protected? It is not my goal here to address in detail the security of information systems and software but to make you realize that security is neither an empty word nor a simple notion. It requires skills and it should be audited by an outside entity to ensure its quality.

Software security flaws

All human work has errors and flaws. No software is free from those errors and flaws. A simple search on the internet about software security flaws brings back thousands of links. Looking for "security update" on the Microsoft, Oracle and Red Hat websites return several hundred articles. No vendor is immune, same for Open Source, despite often contradictory position from proponents of free software. My point is not to oppose open source to proprietary, but to draw

---

[4] McAfee Labs report on the threat landscape:
https://www.mcafee.com/us/resources/reports/rp-quarterly-threats-mar-2017.pdf
[5] https://cloudblogs.microsoft.com/microsoftsecure/2011/02/14/back-to-the-future-attack-surface-analysis-and-reduction/

attention to good practices about management of software security vulnerabilities.

Do you remember Heartbleed[6], back in 2014? This breach of the OpenSSL Protocol impacted millions of web servers, including those of service providers like Facebook, Google or Dropbox. Any user identified on a compromised server was unknowingly at risk because the exploitation of software was undetectable. Once servers have been corrected, users should have proceeded to change their passwords to avoid identity theft.

This incident illustrates two crucial points of information security management: software update and information to users. Regarding the first point, we need to apply security updates as soon as they are made public. We can have a look at the good practice of infrastructure management as described in ITIL (*Information Technology Infrastructure Library*) or the four levels of the Microsoft infrastructure optimization.

	Basic	Standardized	Rationalized	Dynamic
Governance	• No governance • No service level agreement • Ad hoc management of issues and change	• Defined assistance service • Documented incident response policy • Limited management of issues and change	• Defined version management • Documented operations • Defined service levels • Improved configuration management	• Proactive and agile infrastructure • Optimized services engagements • Improved service levels and activity continuity
Security	• Ad hoc management of issues and change • Limited responsibilities • No answers to incidents • Limited access controls	• Limited management of issues and change • Limited risks evaluation • Data protected by passwords • Limited automation	• Defined security compliance and automated audit tools • Documented threat and vulnerabilities • Security standards defined for all software acquisition	• Automated risk monitoring • Managed process for network and data security • Automated auditing of security policies

Figure 2-1 - Microsoft Infrastructure Optimization Models

Assess your data center software vulnerabilities exposure from the above four levels. Data centers from Microsoft, Google, Amazon or OVH, to name a few,

---

[6] Here's an FAQ on cnet.com about Heartbleed:
https://www.cnet.com/news/heartbleed-bug-what-you-need-to-know-faq/

have dynamic infrastructures and security updates are applied as fast as possible to minimize the attack surface. Is it the same in your data center?

Once a vulnerability is known, it's generally exploited on a large scale by hackers. Every single minute that passes between detection and correction is a danger to your users and your data.

Security Information Management Systems

During the implementation of a data center, the Security Information Management System (SIM, Security Information Management, or SIEM, Security Information and Event Management) plays a central place to analyze events in real time, then correlate and draw conclusions on intrusions, intrusion attempts or any security and integrity of the system related events.

These tools are generally based on aggregation, correlation, and analysis of the various event logs. They're therefore useful only once the breach is made. Especially since an intrusion due to identity theft can happen several days or weeks before it is detected by log analysis. The most sophisticated of them are also able to delete the log entries and thus to carry out their attack without leaving detectable traces by the SIM. A Microsoft study shows that a hacker averaged 146 days on a network before being detected. At the opposite, a report from Verizon about computer breaches indicates that an attack to penetrate a system takes only a few seconds, or at worst minutes.

If it is necessary, the SIM isn't sufficient to protect from the sophistication of the current attacks. We need to add a behavioral analysis engine.

Behavioral analysis

To understand why a SIM isn't enough to ensure the security of the information system, we need to understand the general mechanism of an attack.

Figure 2-2 - Schematic of a computer attack

Figure 2-2 describes the principles of an attack. Let's look at those five steps.

1. Identity theft. The hacker needs to break into the network. Regardless of the method used (code injection, pass-the-hash, …), she must succeed in getting a genuine way to enter the network. By stealing an identity, she's guaranteed access without, initially, be detected as an intrusion. It is therefore essential to give users only the minimum rights required for their jobs. It is the policy of least privilege, allowing to minimize Zero-Day attacks, i.e. those for which exist no antiviral signature.

2. Once the identity has been obtained, the hacker will enter the network and will get its mapping by using commands that leave no trace and return this information to its designer to determine the next steps. The next step will be to seek to elevate her privilege to administrator level. If a server is not protected, for example by using the admin-admin or admin-password pair, the hacker using her spoofed identity will seize it and will use it to continue her trip[7].

3. The hacker is now an administrator. She will be able to act with impunity without being worried because, in view of the network, she has all the rights. She will, therefore, begin to collect information and send it back to its designer. She will then be able to decide what she wants to steal, destroy or encrypt, in the event of an attack by ransomware.

4. Theft, destruction or encryption of data can begin. Here again, it is activities carried out by an administrator, who can erase its traces, in the case of the most sophisticated attacks.

5. The data is exposed to the public or used to demand a ransom. The breach is detected then, but too late, the damage being done.

The previously described scheme, unfortunately, is not an invention of the imagination, but one suffered by several organizations every day in the world. McAfee Labs estimates the average number of incidents of data leakage between 11 and 50 per day!

We need to get protection from behavior analysis based on automated machine learning. Behavioral analysis software, if it integrates with the SIM, does not rely

---

[7] McAfee indicates that the delay between intrusion and detection is still increasing. Microsoft estimates it at 146 days, close to five months!

on the event logs but on the behavior of each identity of the directory. It learns, detects and responds.

Let's get back to the previous steps to understand the behavioral analysis detection mechanism.

1. Theft of identity. The compromised user is rarely an administrator. However, even though it would be, based on the segmentation of administrative rights, it doesn't probably have access to the entire network under the concept of least privilege. Therefore, any user has a predictable behavior. Behavioral analysis software discovers and records user's 'normal' paths: their hours of connection, their places of connection, the use of resources, access to applications, etc.

2. The compromised identity is now trying to access resources which it generally does not try to access. The suspicious behavior is detected, and the software now looks closer at this particular identity. If the attack is sophisticated and the hacker wants to limit its exposure to a possible detection, it will also analyze the behavior of the identity he has usurped and will limit his actions in order not to arouse the attention. However, it is important to note that to achieve its mission, the hacker must act "openly" using the identity he has usurped. Insofar as the user whose identity has been compromised will attempt to access resources by raising its privileges, the scanning engine will send one or more alerts to the network administrator or to the SIM, and potentially trigger an action as forcing the change of the password or disabling temporarily the account.

3. The usurper cannot get access to the network anymore as its identity has changed or has been disabled.

It's, as you could see, the unusual behavior of the user who is the base of the intrusion detection before the intruder had time to carry out its mission. The question is, therefore: Is your data center protected by a SIM and some mechanisms of behavior analysis?

As we've just seen it, if security is one of the focal points of your public cloud choice, the question is not so simple and must be studied with a lens on modern threats, with the right management tools. In my discussions with many clients of any size, if the security issue is prominent, his treatment is largely inadequate, leaving the information system exposed to any kind of intrusions.

Yes, but what about the interception of data?

Well, a public cloud data center is certainly more secure than mine, but at least I control my network and I have no need to go through a Web link that can be spied.

For sure, it has been proven that a hacker can probably play the "man in the middle" and intercept all communications through an optical fiber (even simpler and cheaper with copper). Now, two rational arguments:

- If a hacker wants your information, it will be quicker for him to attempt an intrusion that to intercept megabytes of encrypted communications (it goes without saying that no clear communication must be made to or from the data center).
- The hacker will require large computing power and storage. He will indeed have to store data to be able to treat and eliminate the noise, i.e. communications that do not interest him. Once stored, he will need to decrypt it and breaking a key requires huge computing power that few have, outside of big country's intelligence agencies.

Unless you don't work for an overly sensitive sector requiring high levels of confidentiality and potential target of remarkably equipped cyber terrorists, there is little chance that your information is intercepted. Go back to the attack surfaces and ask yourself the question of interception from the point of view of a threat to curb. You will have to discuss with the provider of your virtual private network between your organization and the data center, like those of Microsoft with ExpressRoute or OBS with Cloud Ready.

To close this question, we need to acknowledge it is totally legitimate following Edward Snowden's revelations, Wikileaks and the many cases of information theft. However, it is important to note that in most of the cases, information is not intercepted, but stolen from an intrusion in the network done with a spoofed identity. If you fear the interception of your data on an encrypted network, can you first be certain that your information system is completely impenetrable?

Bandwidth

The second big question concerning the adoption of cloud technologies is bandwidth. It is obvious that between a gigabit network connection to the company's servers and that of a few megabits of an internet connection, there is a difference in performance and potentially cost.

But again, as with many other subjects, everything is, on the one hand, an infrastructure issue and on the other hand a usage one. Let's take a few examples to illustrate my point.

One location and sedentary employees

Let's say your organization is located in one place and all employees work there, without ever having to move. The calculation is simple: Is it more expensive to have its data center locally or to subscribe to a public cloud by maintaining a quick connection? All you must do is add up the costs of acquiring and maintaining the hardware and software and compare it with those of the bandwidth rentals needed to operate the same hardware and software in the cloud.

If more and more SME chose the cloud, it's because it's worth it. Ask a Nigerian company how much its generator costs in terms of the acquisition, maintenance and use per kilowatt/hour and compare to what your energy provider invoices you. The financial logic goes toward service pooling. I have taken the Nigeria example because its energy network is one of the worst in Africa and that it is, for the moment, almost impossible to rely only on an official energy provider (from the EIA – *Energy Information Administration, eia.gov* – 30% of electricity in Nigeria is produced by private generators).

Just like, producing your own electricity or purifying your water would not even be considered as an option, more and more organizations are choosing to no longer invest money in servers and the infrastructure that goes with it. Thus, even if the situation of a single location and of sedentary employees can make them think, there is a strong bet that the simple financial calculation is favorable to the cloud, as in the example given in Figure 2-3.

10 Entry Level Virtual Machines in a public cloud		10 Entry Level Servers in a private cloud	
10 standard Virtual Machines, A2 (2 cores,		Hardware (10 servers, RAID array, UPS,	
3.5GB of RAM, 135GB HDD, $0.304/hr	$ 1,129.35	Backup)	$ 749.44
1TB/month	$ 74.76	Support	$ 599.72
Internet Connexion 50Mbps	$ 46.38	Power	$ 120.96
Support	$ 252.99	Internet Connexion	$ 90.00
Monthly Total	$ 1,503.48	Monthly Total	$ 1,560.12

Figure 2-3 - Simple comparison between a local solution and in the cloud

The example of Figure 2-3 is evaluated from the public prices of HP and Microsoft. They are purely indicative, tax-free and without software. The idea is to compare an installation of 10 enterprise servers and their equivalent in the cloud, taking into account the necessary bandwidth increase. The cost of the equipment considers a monthly depreciation over 36 months.

It is always difficult to compare two models only on a financial side. In addition, we can criticize the choice of comparing 10 virtual servers with 10 entry-level physical servers, while it could have been done in relation to a more powerful server for hosting 10 virtual servers. Still, we would have had to cluster it if we want to achieve the fault tolerance of the machines in the cloud. If there is no directly comparable solution, their usage charges are comparable and that is what matters to us here.

One location and mobile employees

Now consider that some of your employees are mobile. For example, your salespeople, your maintenance technicians or your consultants. They need to connect to your data center to access applications, such as e-mail, customer relationship management, or inventory.

So, we'll have to set up a VPN connection, ensure that the applications work in a remote mode and have two connection modes: local and remote. If now all applications are in a public cloud, whether you are local or remote, you will probably connect to it in the same way, either with a remote workstation to save bandwidth or in web mode, as more and more modern applications allow it.

So of course, arises the question of what happens if the Internet connection falls. I come back to this question in Chapter 3, Urban Legends. But, apart from this question, the advantage goes to the cloud.

Several locations away from tens, hundreds or thousands of kilometers

This configuration, standard for multinational organizations and ones with multiple agencies, demands more architectural analysis. It happens that beyond security and connection availability, the architecture is set up as a hub and spokes and that only one internet access point is available at the hub level. The hub becomes the bottleneck and a cloud solution will require a more careful planning. Like I use to tell customers: if the public cloud was the panacea, we would not have invented the hybrid cloud! Every situation is unique, it calls for unique solutions.

However, the challenge of mobile employees needs to be addressed if we are to improve productivity. And there, cloud technologies generally do not have an on-premises equivalent and cannot compare with setting up specialized connections or a virtual private network.

To close this topic on the bandwidth, the experience showed me four key points:

- A thorough study of the network infrastructure is necessary to understand the information flow and identify potential bottlenecks. Do not embark on a public cloud project until you have upgraded the network topology and its routing. We will come back to this point in Chapter 5, Best Practices.
- The necessary bandwidth is directly dependent on the used services and always undersized by the service providers. Multiply it all by two and you will not be far from reality!
- A thorough study of network and Internet data flows must be conducted before embarking on the implementation of public or hybrid cloud services. All organizations are different, and no off-the-shelf recommendations can be the true truth.
- The solution is always hybrid, unless you have a true pure vision of the public cloud and want to go all-in, in which case the connection to the data center becomes the critical point to study.

Real and hidden costs

In the example illustrated in Figure 2-3, the advantage went by a short head to the cloud. This is neither always the case, nor always that simple. Yet one of the arguments of public cloud providers is financial and it is often unstoppable. So, to get a more precise idea, let's look at the magnifying glass with some advanced arguments in favor of the cloud.

I only pay for what I use, so it's cheaper

This is the principle of car rental or carpooling, and in general, all rental offers. The calculation is simple. You take the cost of acquiring the equipment, its cost of management and maintenance, its amortization on the duration of use and compare it over the same period to the renting of the same equipment according to your needs.

For the services you only use a few times a month, this can have a certain economic advantage. For example, launching a series of calculations for a marketing study can require a lot of power just for a few days. On the other hand, for the services you can use at any time, such as e-mail or file storage, comparing the price per mailbox can be detrimental to the cloud.

One of the constraints of IT is often the hardware and software acquisition required for the solution we need. There's, therefore, a fixed cost, almost independent of the number of users. Hence, we get a result that graphically shows in Figure 2-4, visually favorable to the cloud.

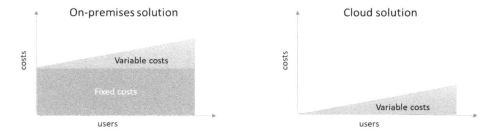

Figure 2-4 - Classic Cost comparison

However, there are two errors in the reasoning:

1. There are not always variable costs to a local solution. In fact, you can acquire hardware and software at a given price, including maintenance, which will cover the needs of the company for many years, including considering the increase in staff. The cost can, therefore, be considered fixed regardless of the number of users.
2. There may be fixed costs to a cloud solution. Indeed, the increase in bandwidth often required is a cost incurred by the organization every month regardless of the number of users. Likewise, a virtual machine can form a fixed monthly cost if this is the solution chosen.

You can then have a completely different scheme.

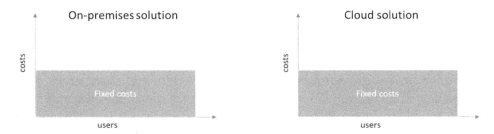

Figure 2-5 - Fixed Cost Solutions

It's also possible to have variable costs in the cloud that increases faster than anticipated, depending on chosen options. They may rapidly go over those of the on-premises solution.

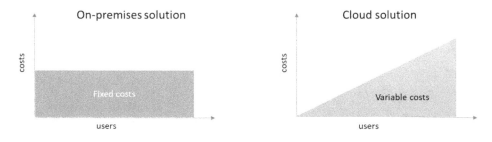

Figure 2-6 - Explosive variable costs

At this same game comparisons, we often compare amortized purchases to running costs. With the cloud, everything goes into running costs, no depreciation, no cash to use to buy a new solution. More and more equipment suppliers propose rental offers that avoid depreciation. Once again, if the benefit seems to go at first glance to the cloud, it may not, depending on the relationships you have with your hardware vendors.

The argument of "I pay for what I use, therefore it's cheaper", does not always work. You need to look into the details of the licensing model. It's often complex and sometimes makes the comparison just impossible.

I no longer need IT staff

It will not please IT people: we do not need you anymore! We moved everything to the cloud! Thank you for your contribution! Moving all or partially your IT in the cloud does not kill all the IT infrastructure and therefore the need for IT personnel.

An example, among others, except if you do not need to print anything concerns the print server and the printers. You may need a local server and a local network to print locally. There will also some legacy applications that will not be able to move and will require a local authentication server. And there will be all the local support requirements due to a failed network, a lost file, etc.

There's also the IT system evolution. With a detailed invoicing, we can precisely measure how much each user costs. It's, therefore, possible to transform the IT department into a profit center so that each department knows exactly how much IT consumes. Why do I go this route? To let you know that the role of the IT personnel is changing but not completely disappearing. The move to the cloud can be used to outsource more functions, this is another discussion. However, IT is becoming measurable and potentially « profitable », it can be a force to transform the organization, as we will see in Chapter 6, Opportunities.

So, before you scratch one or more wages from your payroll, think twice about it.

My employees will become more productive

On paper, yes, in reality, no. I'm thought-provoking, but barely. In a clear majority of cloud projects I've seen in the last four years, the deployment of the new technology faced massive user resistance.

This takes several forms: from the inability of management to decide who should benefit from the new tools to set aside these tools for fear of "policing" by management. So, if the provider promises you the moon and a stellar increase in employee productivity, talk to him about change management. There is a strong bet that this issue will lead to long and insightful discussions.

However, two numbers should make you think. From the Microsoft's experience, a cloud project without change management succeeds in only 15% of the cases! Yes, you read well, 15%! Frightening! To the opposite, the success rate goes to 84% when change management is part of the project. Six times the rate of success. This is moving from failure to success. The purpose of this book is not to go into the details of change management, there are many books and consulting firms whose job it is, that will be more than happy to assist you.

Start with the principle that change is scary for most people. As Robin Sharma said: "change is hard at the beginning, messy in the middle and gorgeous at the end". It's crucial to go through those steps with trust and to be therefore assisted. Allow me to provide some advice on what to do to successfully adopt cloud technologies.

I use the ADKAR[8] methodology (https://www.prosci.com/adkar/adkar-model) of the company Prosci that I saw at work and noted the fantastic results. ADKAR is the acronym of Awareness, Desire, Knowledge, Ability, and Reinforcement.

- Raise the **Awareness** of the reasons for the change. This is internal communication. Explain why change is necessary, its goals and its positive outcome for employees.
- Create the **Desire** to participate and engage in the process of change. The management oversees instilling the desire for change in order to reduce the resistance.
- Acquire the **Knowledge** by getting trained on the usage of the new tools.
- Achieve the level of performance by developing the **Ability** to use the new tools and processes.

---

[8] You can download a free ebook on the method, in English, here: http://empower.prosci.com/the-prosci-adkar-model-ebook

- **Reinforce** knowledge and ability to anchor change in a sustainable way, through support and corrective measures if necessary.

Nothing revolutionary as you can see, but an organized and sensible approach. The crucial point is to bring the employees into this change, not impose it on them.

By adopting these five steps to the implementation of a new technology, it gives us the following elements:

- **Awareness**: Explain each new tool, its features, its security, the differences with the current situation and especially the benefits for everyone. This can range from using mail to file sharing to phone calls, to dashboards. The important thing is to implement a steering committee in which employees are involved.
- **Desire**: The key point in creating the desire for change is the establishment of referent employees. These referents will play a key role in the extent to which they will actively accompany the upcoming change. They are the confidantes, the coaches, the stooges of change, the people to whom we go to understand, to apprehend, to adopt the change.
- **Knowledge**. Training is key. If it's not enough, it's necessary. If the tools got simpler over the years and the notion of application is now common, the adoption of a new tool, a new software, new processes requires training. Online, in the classroom or a mix of both, it's necessary and needs to be measured.
- **Ability**. The difference between knowledge and ability is application. Is knowledge applied? Does it lead to change in functioning? Did it help achieve productivity goals? Ability is measured daily and must include the whole of management.
- **Reinforce**. Referent must remind employees, explain the new features, allow to erase lingering doubts. The objective is to anchor the new technologies in the functioning of the organization and to make that everyone can measure the positive implications, or even correct the negative ones.

Now, if the technology lands smoothly, the effects will soon be felt:

- Possibility to implement a teleworking policy, both in terms of tools and processes.
- Secure use of personal devices.
- Ease and speed of implementation of new processes.
- Acceleration the transformation of the organization

All this may seem trivial, but the experience shows it's not. Change management can help in landing the new organizational strategy and benefits both the organization and the employee. When technology is not explained and adopted, negative consequences are numerous, starting with useless expenditures. The following two imperatives need to be reconciled :

- Implement the technologies necessary for the development of the organization.
- Ensure the safety and adherence to the compliance rules.

This cannot be achieved without the involvement of the staff and without a structured approach. It is at this price that "your employees will become more productive".

Cloud and "Green IT"

IT consumes a lot of energy. But what is not today? Most human activities consume electricity or gas. IT does too. "Green IT" or "Green Computing », has even its Wikipedia page (https://en.wikipedia.org/wiki/Green_computing), which somehow proves its importance.

I will not try to answer if the cloud is environmentally sustainable. However, between my on-premises datacenter and those of my cloud provider, which is greener? In the end, wherever I will run my apps, I will need energy (it's here out of question to totally get rid of IT).

Some proven facts to begin with:

1. According to Greenpeace, data centers consume 2% of the world's energy.

2. The Power Usage Effectiveness (PUE) continues to decrease to now reach 1.1. This means 0.1 kilowatt is necessary to produce 1 kilowatt of IT used energy.
3. According to the World Bank, the cost of electricity in Africa is on average double that of international standards, due to the preponderant share of oil thermal power plants, the low usage of hydraulic capacity and the high frequency of diesel generators.
4. The major players are engaged in renewable energies, most having a plan to reach 100% of renewables by 2020.
5. According to a study by Accenture and WSP Energy, a company decreases its carbon footprint by 30%, on average, by moving from local IT services to cloud services, and up to 90% in the case of SMEs.
6. The tolerable temperature and humidity inside the servers have increased over the years to decrease the air conditioning requirements.

I could continue on and on. However, one critical point for the African continent remains the IT carbon footprint. I am still to meet a customer with a carbon footprint reduction strategy. Electricity, its usage, production, and source, is not a factor of choice of a computing solution. This is mostly due to the lack of political and industrial incentive to use green power.

However, with a very high cost of electricity and a below-the-average electricity quality, the cloud is an alternative that can become very economical from a simple "electrical" point of view. Consider a small data center, consisting of a dozen servers and a few terabytes of storage. In addition to the UPS requirements and possibly a diesel generator, it will consume about nine thousand kilowatts/hour (hundred watts per hour and per machine that can run twenty-four by seven), that is just over two thousand dollars of electricity to which you need to add the same for light and air conditioning. The PUE of a local data center is indeed estimated at 2!

As we see in the previous calculation, in three or four years, we will spend more electricity to run our data center than the initial server investment. And this is only a low estimate because if, as in Nigeria for example, this data center is exclusively powered by a diesel generator, we will be able to multiply these costs by two or three.

Let's stop for a moment on those electrical considerations. From a purely economic and ecological point of view, maintaining a local data center has no logic. However, and this is where the rubber hits the road, electrical costs and the premises usage are part of the overhead that the bookkeeping rarely cross charges to business units. Thus, the IT BU, usually responsible for the operation of the data center, does not see these costs appear in its budget. This is therefore not a topic to be discussed. End of the discussion!

The famous total cost of ownership, compliance with the ISO 14001 standard as well as the environmental pressures from public authorities are to be taken into account seriously. We still need to discuss those beyond the IT: finance and legal need to be involved.

I may upset IT managers and CIOs, but the electrical, environmental and regulatory footprint of a local data center must be considered and quantified. This will allow determining objectively whether keeping the data center on premises makes sense. The goal is not to take power away from IT, but to allow it to control its own destiny.

So, is the cloud "green"? If the controversy will continue to fuel the blogosphere and the debates between pro and anti will continue, we can only see a trend towards more renewable energy, ecological design and taking into account the ecological footprint. The awareness of the electricity consumption of the cloud and globally of data centers had a positive impact on technologies. From the 48-volt DC power supply to the server design to minimize consumption and promote recycling, from air circulation to cool machines to the usage of heat released to heat public buildings, from the generalization of virtualization to adherence to standards, the cloud providers accelerate the movement to make their data center as "green" as possible. Of course, this does not go fast enough. Usage of coal or oil to power the data centers is still prevailing and certainly transparency is not always total, but it is important to note that all the major actors are working to reduce their carbon footprint and make their data centers totally "renewable". Here are a few:

- Microsoft: https://www.microsoft.com/about/csr/environment/carbon/operations/
- Google: https://www.google.com/about/datacenters/renewable/index.html

- Salesforce: http://www.salesforce.com/company/sustainability/
- Amazon: https://aws.amazon.com/about-aws/sustainability/
- Ovh: https://www.ovh.com/world/about-us/green-it.xml

You can find many other examples online. The important thing to note here is that the movement has really taken off and nothing really seems to be able to stop it. So, if you are concerned about environmental issues or wish to preempt green legislation, the cloud is a way to green your IT infrastructure. Have a look at the ISO 14001 standard and set up a steering committee to see how to comply.

Limitations and constraints of the cloud

3. Urban legends

« As the human being advances in life, the novel that, young man, dazzled him, the fabulous legend that, as a child, seduced him, fade and darken by themselves. »

Artificial Paradises, Charles Baudelaire.

If the cloud is not the panacea for all the IT challenges of any business, it is one of the indispensable elements of the IT strategy today. Looking beyond IT, it is the business strategy that is currently being discussed, cloud technologies can provide flexibility and agility.

However, the positive sides cannot fully enlighten the less shiny sides of the constraints that we have previously seen. Now, because any change is difficult, misinformation, FUD (*Fear, Uncertainty, Doubt*) and poor understanding of technology have the effect of creating "urban legends" about these technologies. Certainly, behind any legend, there is sometimes a truth. In addition, no technology is errors, faults and imperfections free. It's not because your fuel tank can explode, and your car catch fire that you're going to leave your car in the garage. The same goes for the cloud. If we have to have a pragmatic approach and weigh the pros and cons, it is not a question of throwing the baby out with the bathwater.

So let's look at four urban legends that are well constantly heard *ad nauseam* with almost every client today:

- Security is paramount, and the cloud is not secure.
- The government/regulator does not allow me to use cloud technologies.
- If I move my data center and my applications into the cloud, I lose control of my IT.
- Once everything is in the cloud, if my Internet connection fails, I can no longer work.

The cloud is not secure

"With all those stories of data loss and leakage, you see that the cloud is not secure!" It is obvious that WikiLeaks, Russian online involvement in the American presidential campaign and many other stories does not help the impression that the cloud is secure. Now, of course, media are not interested in the billions of transactions happening safely every day, but only by the ones that will create a great cover story. Where does come from this feeling that the cloud is not secure and that, *de facto*, my data is safer when stored locally?

Let's start with some statistics to support this feeling. According to a June 2016 study from IBM and the Ponemon Institute:

- The average cost of data theft is four million dollars.
- This cost is increasing by 29% compared to 2013.
- 48% of data thefts are pirate's work – 37% in South Africa – the remainder is due either to human errors or to system errors.

Let's add more!

- According to NetIQ, 70% of companies interviewed have been the victims of a cyber-attack in 2014.

- According to Verizon, nearly 80% of successful attacks involves a server or a personal computer.
- Still, according to Verizon, the intrusion time in the network is only a few minutes and the actual data last a few days.

Shall I stop? You'll find tons and tons of other stories and statistics on the internet. So, what is the result? Lock you up in your house, pull the curtains, disconnect from the internet and wait for the end of the world... Of course, impossible and not desirable! Finally, one last statistic, mine: 100% of the clients who were certain to be totally safe, had one or more exploitable flaws. No one, I say it well and I repeat, no one is safe from a security breach.

To almost definitively get rid of this urban legend, let's go back to the base of any open systems interconnection, the OSI model.

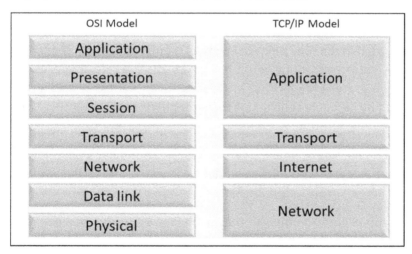

Figure 3-1 - OSI and TCP-IP models

The OSI model (*Open Systems Interconnection*) describes the required functionalities to communicate between computers. Supplanted in the eighties by the TCP/IP model, the foundation of the Internet, it always serves as a reference to discussions about communication between computers. We should also extrapolate the word computer to any connected object. With the Internet of Things (IoT), we cannot compare a connected object to computer, although its connection to the Internet or to a private network uses the same technological bricks.

Why returning to these basic elements? To bring the concept of defense in depth to the front of the scene, consisting in securing all components of a system. Let's consider a few common-sense questions:

- Why bothering installing a firewall that filters network access if passwords are not the subject of any policy?
- Why bothering securing physical access to the data center if data are stored in plaintext, without encryption, on hard disks?
- Why bothering implementing two-factor authentication if the Web servers are not patched and allow SQL code to be injected into the database?
- Why bothering adding anti-virus and anti-malware if mobile devices that access applications from the Internet are not subject to security policy forcing them to use the latest security patches?

I could go on, but I think you understand the purpose of defense in depth. I usually summarize it in the following way: why bothering installing a reinforced door, adding an alarm and putting your precious effects in a safe, if you leave a window open while going on vacation? The security of a network and a data center is defined by its weakest link, as is the strength of a steel chain!

Now that we have asked these few common-sense questions and put back on the table the OSI and TCP/IP models, can you make an honest assessment of your data center to each layer of the model and compare it to that of your potential cloud service provider's data center?

I can bet that you will not be able to match the security level of the service provider. Just start by looking at the certifications that the provider is complying with. However, I am proposing the following seven elements to make an objective comparison:

- Physical access to the data center: access control, monitoring, alarm...
- Physical protection of data: resistance to disasters (water, fire...), data redundancy, response procedure in case of theft...
- Logical access to the network: password policy, access control, access rights, filtering (user, application, hardware), logging...

- Monitoring, protection, and detection: intrusion detection, intrusion prevention, and intrusion response systems, packet monitoring firewall, anti-virus, anti-malware update...
- Independent Audit and Certification: annual security audit by a trusted third party, attempted intrusion (white hacking) ...
- Business continuity procedures: hot and cold recovery sites, recovery or business continuity plan, software update procedures...
- End-to-end encryption: encryption of communications and stored data, the introduction of digital certificates...

You can make a two-column table for each of the previous items by listing what you have in local and what the provider offers you as standard or optional. These lists are generally rich in learning and will help you to decide in all honesty which of your data center or that of your provider is the most secure. The best is often the enemy of the good, as loved to repeat my physics teacher, but no one is no longer immune to information piracy. Whatever the industry in which you work, your customers will never like the information you store about them to be exposed to the public, and you will never like to expose your company's information to the public, whatever they may be.

So is the cloud secure? The final word goes to the CEO of a large bank on his way out of the Microsoft data center visit of Quincy, one of the world's largest: "I now understand why the bank's data may be safer here than the gold in our safe".

The law forbids me to use the cloud

After security, this is the second urban legend put forward to justify the on-premises choice. Whether it is the central government or the regulatory body, like the central bank, there is always a culprit to blame. The question then is: "And you can share the legislation in question?" To which, the answer is almost always invariably: "No, but we will seek." The research is then worthy of the discussion between Alice and the Cheshire cat because in most cases this law or rule simply generally does not exist.

I detail later the legislation questions, both local and international, in terms of storing data in the cloud. However, to twist the neck of this urban legend, it is necessary to begin to ask the question of what actions are performed in the cloud and particularly involving the data.

Let's have a look at some interesting cases of cloud utilization:

- **The institutional website**. The data is public, since accessible by everyone. There is, of course, confidential data that no well-meaning person will put online. In the meantime, this is the essence of the cloud.
- **Software updates**. If your machine is connected to a network, there is a strong bet that it is used to exchange information and therefore uses the Internet. Since software bugs exist, it is necessary to update it regularly. There is a good chance that this update will be automatic and will happen in the background without you even being aware. Impossible to escape unless you want to increase the risk of intrusion.
- If you work in the bank and insurance, you will need to make powerful calculations to make estimates of credit risk or carry out actuarial calculations. The availability of powerful virtual machines dedicated to calculation from anonymized data is an incredible asset.
- **Multi-factor authentication**. Whether it is for your employees or for the users of your services, it becomes essential to strengthen access security using multifactor authentication. If biometrics, fingerprints or facial recognition begin to be integrated into many devices, it is not generalized and therefore cannot be the only method of strengthening the security of access to services they are local or online. Authentication by SMS or by a smartphone application is then the solution that works in 100% of the cases: you must enter a code received by SMS or through an application that runs on your smartphone. What could be more natural than using an existing cloud service to generate these codes?
- **Trend, fraud or deviation detection**. The cloud allows you to get access to artificial intelligence to learn from and apply complex heuristics to your data models. All data can (must) be made anonymous to ensure full confidentiality, and then can be used to detect in real-time these model deviations that may mean a reversal of a trend or possibility of a fraud, in the case of a bank for example. This requires an important computing power and access to these artificial intelligences that few companies have the means to develop internally.

- **Bots and social networking services**. Do you want to enable a 24x7 customer service or manage the customer's queues in an efficient way? A bot is a perfect answer. On top of these, they can interact in multiple languages! The quality of the bots has considerably increased in recent years and if they cannot, yet, completely replace a human operator, they form an excellent complement.

So, does the law forbid any of the services discussed here with which no users, citizens or employees' data are stored in the cloud? Probably not. And this is a crucial point to consider! If the doubt may persist about the legislation in force; If the impression of the relative security of on-premises storage is understandable; if data sovereignty cannot be discussed; cloud services are not always synonymous to end-user data storage but always to faster implementation and access to compute power or excessively costly, if not impossible, services to be implemented in a local datacenter.

So yes, we can ask the question of the hegemony of the few major providers like Google, Facebook, Amazon or Microsoft in the field of artificial intelligence or enjoy it, while complying with the law.

With the cloud, I lose control

How reassuring these LEDs that flash in my data center are! They have this unique ability to give the impression of human control over the machine. If a machine stops, I can change it. If I have a network problem, I can intervene at the router and hub level. If a disk fails, I can change it. I'm in control of my computer.

Model	Cost	Scalability	Hardware control	Data control
On-premises private cloud	High	Limited	Total	Total
Hosted private cloud	Medium	Limited	Medium	Total
Public cloud	Low	Unlimited	Limited	Total

Figure 3-2 - Cloud models and control

Total control comes at a very high cost that fewer and fewer organizations can maintain but comes mainly with extremely limited scalability and flexibility. With the explosion of data and the increasing reliance on artificial intelligence, organizations are confronted with a growing need for storage and computational power. However, this has an increasingly high cost of both material and structure. Hosting at a provider does not necessarily change the deal, except by pooling some costs, but at the expense of loss of control over the equipment.

The public cloud is the only solution with low cost and almost unlimited scalability. But what control do we really have on our computers environment? On the hardware, the control is limited but sufficient in most cases. What do you have choices on?

- The type of virtual machine. You can choose the type of machine depending on the type of process you want to carry.
- The location of this machine. Some providers allow you to choose the data center that will host your machine. Others don't. Pay attention to the jurisdiction used, I will go into those details in Chapter 4, Legislation.
- What you do with this machine. You can stop it, restart it, or reinstall it as you please, and get rid of it when you no longer need it.
- The software you install (IaaS). You install what you want as long as the virtual machine supports it.

What do you have no choice on?

- The acquisition of the equipment. You do not buy the computer but use it. The specifications are therefore chosen by the provider. However, in most cases, the hardware is more optimized than conventional equipment.
- Software update In Saas or PaaS, the software used is usually the latest versions, patched continuously.
- The location of this machine. Some providers do not allow you to choose the data center that will host your machine or your treatment. They use the closest data center to your organization. This choice is not always wise for a question of jurisdiction as we will see in Chapter 4, Legislation.

If you keep some of the control on your machines, there are also elements that you no longer need to worry about and that frees your time and energy:

- The acquisition of the equipment. No need to shop around, bid and receive the order. With all the problems that may be attached to it: non-compliant material, damaged in transport, defective...
- Hardware maintenance. Increasing memory, changing the network card or hard disks, or dusting are actions of the past.
- Hardware configuration. Servers setup, installation, and tuning of the software are also actions of the past.
- Software updates. Anti-malware, security patch, operating system upgrades are left in the hands of the cloud provider.

Basically, you are no longer concerned with piping and boilers, but can you focus on the value added to the organization through IT services and processing. So, in the end, do you lose control over your computer? In the same way that you have lost control over changing the oil of your car engine with the advent of computers in cars. This does not take away the use of the car, but increases its reliability, availability and allows you to devote yourself to something else. And if you like mechanics, no one keeps you from spending the weekend on it, but not with your work tool.

This change of control has an important effect on the IT teams: they change jobs. Goodbye to hardware and software management, hello to strategy, the involvement of the personnel and the focus of the business. It is no longer a matter of indulging in the technicality of the tool but in its real contribution to the company. With the cloud, the power has changed hands. It is between those of the users now.

No Internet, no work

"My good sir, all your cloud is pretty, but if I have no connection, it is useless!" This argument always makes me smile so much. At first glance, it's logical and common sense. You can also apply it to electricity, to heating in the winter, to gasoline for cars and all these services and goods that we need to work and depend on.

It is quite clear that the use of cloud technologies increases our dependence on a broadband internet connection. This is usually why we are trying to diversify the sources of connections and make them redundant.

A bit like owning a diesel generator in countries where the electrical supply is unreliable. Travel to Nigeria to see the presence of diesel generators at the foot of all buildings.

To this argument of internet dependence, I, therefore, asked the question of the availability rate of these famous connections. One small question: "What has been the cumulative duration of the unavailability of your Internet connection in the last twelve months?" And I generally wait in vain... No statistics, no numbers, nothing tangible, just an impression.

So, I ask the second question that annoys: "Over the last twelve months, what has been the cumulative duration of the unavailability of your network or data center". Again, I often wait in vain. And then sometimes I heard that yes, maybe the on-premises services were less available than the Internet.

The facts are as follows:

- Public cloud data centers have availability rates near and sometimes higher than 99.9%. This corresponds to less than 52 minutes of downtime per year ... 52 minutes, less than 9 seconds per day on average.
- Professional Internet connection offers have close availability rates and sometimes higher than 99.9%. I'm not doing the math again.

So of course, we still see most of companies using a consumer ADSL Internet connection without any service level agreement. From the moment there is a dependency on a service, the tools and the means necessary for its maximum availability should be put in place. Again, the IT job is changing. A local area network (LAN) maintenance does not require the same skills as the maintenance of a wide Internet network (WAN). The jungle of Internet offers, and sometimes the stranglehold on the network by a handful of providers, does not make easy, and sometimes economical, the connection choices.

The number one rule is to completely review its Internet connection mode. All telecom operators and Internet service providers offer IP VPN (Virtual private network) circuits that increase the security and reliability of your data center connections in the cloud. It is also possible to consider a routed private network-to provider data center like AWS Direct Connect or Azure ExpressRoute.

ExpressRoute, Direct Connect, and VLAN

These services, respectively, from Microsoft and Amazon, are nothing else but virtual LANs (VLANs), following the IEEE 802.1q standard. The idea is to establish a redundant and secure direct link between your local network and the entry point of the data center hosting the subscribed services, to improve its reliability.

Attention, this connection is no longer an Internet connection. It does not allow access to the Internet, but only to the services of the provider (Microsoft or Amazon in this case). It will, therefore, be appropriate to have an additional Internet connection to allow access to other services. This can bear extra costs.

Now it is necessary to look at the interconnection mechanisms as a whole. In fact, public cloud services are seen by the end user as if they were running locally. In fact, the user does not care about the location of the processing of these services. What interests him is to be able to access it in the most transparent way possible. A VLAN makes it possible to create a completely transparent hybrid cloud. As the name implies, it is a "local" network even if the data center is thousands of kilometers from your organization.

Thus, even from Nairobi or Abidjan, a VLAN connection to a data center in Ireland or India makes it "local". Again, the choice of such a connection and its speed depends on the used services. Making the choice, however, makes it possible to implement many management tools designed for hybrid datacenters. This allows you ultimately to take advantage of the best of both worlds: the total control of a local data center and the power and flexibility of a public cloud data center.

When choosing a "cast-iron" connection, VLAN or something else, let's look at what happens if this connection fails. First thing first: The Earth continues to spin. Whatever happens to your connection, your computer is working, your local data is still there and your ability to work remains almost intact. Take the example of messaging: your messages are in a local cache (forget the exclusive use of an Internet Explorer to take your e-mail messages and turn to a rich client) so you can continue to read and send them. the latter will remain in your outbox until your connection returns.

It can be the same with your files or any other important document or application that you must have access to even when there is no connection. So obviously, what about the CRM or the ERP, or any other application that requires a connection?

The question arises obviously but is especially suitable to be looked at in terms of quality of service. The first question I ask often is: "Over the last twelve months, how long has your Internet connection been unavailable?" usually no statistics. So, I propose to do a small study from now on and for the next thirty days. The second question is: "Over the last twelve months, how long have your critical applications been unavailable?" Here again often no statistics. But when you ask users, local applications are often more unavailable than the Internet connection. Not always the case, no statistics to prove it, but the questions are worth asking because they generate a background reflection on the quality of service both locally and remotely.

Any professional Internet connection provider has a quality of service commitment. When you depend on a permanent connection – and unless you live in total self-sufficiency, you will depend more and more on it – a contingency plan should be put in place: using a VSAT degraded link, using a WiMax or GSM fallback link, use of another provider, etc. The two important points being:

1. Plan it and document it
2. Set up communication with users

There will be problems. The difference in experience for the end user will be in the way you manage them.

I end this last urban legend on an important point: our dependence on the Internet is only growing and inescapable. This leads to a significant increase in the reliability and hence the redundancy of the links. Just see the Figure 3-3 - Submarine cables in 2005 and projection in 2018. Until 2009, Africa was irrigated only by SAT3/SAFE and 800 Gb. The World Cup in 2010 in South Africa was the trigger to increase connection capacity. And since then, it has been growing with the different cables that have been setup on both the East and West coasts.

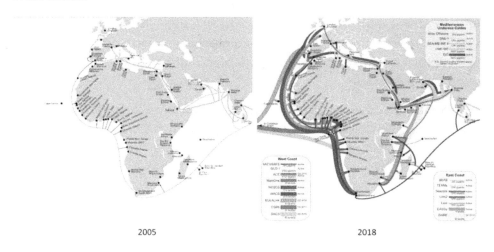

2005   2018

Figure 3-3 - Submarine cables in 2005 and projection in 2018

At the same time, big cities are getting fibered, as are the landlocked countries, such as Botswana or Rwanda to name but two. Certainly, there is still a lot to do, especially in the remote towns and villages. However, increasing bandwidth projects are on the rise: there is the connection by radio waves using the television white space, projects in which Microsoft and Google are involved, in Kenya, South Africa and Ghana in particular. Another project, that of the satellite connection by Facebook and Eutelsat, although the latter underwent a setback due to the explosion of the rocket Falcon 9 of SpaceX which was due to set the satellite in orbit.

All these projects saw access to the Internet increasing significantly: bandwidth increases, while the prices per kilobit decrease and access increases. An important point to note also is the access in 3 or 4G, mainly in cities and on the major areas. Again, with the increasing access to cheap smartphones, access to the network of networks is quickly democratized.

Conclusion

An urban legend is a rumor that spreads rapidly and sounds like truth. In the context of cloud technologies, the four urban legends I have described in the previous pages mostly echo the fear of the unknown. They also use concepts that are not well known. IT security is complex and the explosion of malware, whose proliferation goes through the Internet contributes to the amalgamation of cloud and insecurity.

I often make the parallel between the fear of the airplane and the perceived insecurity of the cloud. Logically and statistically, there are more car crashes than airplane's, but emotionally, a plane crash is more "serious". Logically and statistically, a data or application is more secure in a public cloud datacenter, but emotionally, hacking Yahoo accounts or attacking Liberia is more "serious".

The Achilles heel of the cloud is the Internet connection. Just like the distribution of electricity or water. A leak, a faulty transformer or a line break causes a stop or limitations of the distribution. It is the same with the Internet. For a long time, companies have learned to manage the risk of breakdown of distribution: water tank, emergency power generator. It is possible to do the same with the Internet: emergency VSAT Network, use of the 4G network, geo-replication...

In the end, we can legitimately ask ourselves the question of our dependence on the Internet. All facets of the economy are increasingly dependent on it. Going against its use by developing local data centers is an economic aberration. Like any new technology, the cloud carries a set of fears and risks. We have to learn how to silence them.

In four sentences, the conclusion of these four urban legends:

- The cloud is no less secure than a local network, it is the human mistakes and ignorance that weakens it.
- No law prohibits the use of the cloud, it regulates it and must define the classification of the data.
- Control is a very personal concept that puts IT back to what it is: a means to an end, not an end.

- The Internet connection is the weak link, we need to solidify it by setting up redundancy and offline operation.

Urban legends

4. Legislation

« It is precisely because the force of things always tends to destroy equality, that the force of legislation must always strive to maintain it. »

The social contract, Jean-Jacques Rousseau

Ignorance of the law is no excuse is a principle which also applies to the digital world. The latter also required a plethora of new regulations and laws to protect individuals and businesses. However, laws should not be used to regulate only by limiting what individuals and companies can do in the cloud but also to facilitate and promote digital agility.

This is the case in many countries. Some understand the power that derives from digital, rather than to fight it. Like any technology, it must be regulated, closing the door to abuse. If Europe and the United States have a well-established legal framework, it is not the same in many African countries, as well as a majority of the so-called emerging economies. Their legal framework

85

is at worst non-existent, or in the workings, but rarely, at the time of writing this book, hundred percent complete.

It is therefore important to consider the cloud with a legal and legislative prism. I'll look at six key areas: data sovereignty, its protection, its safety, its privacy, intellectual property, and finally, the notion of contract which describes these concepts and define the rights and duties of each party.

As we are in a chapter on law, allow me a few words of caution. The law is complex and constantly evolving. This chapter would need to be developed into a full-fledged book to try to be as comprehensive as possible. It forms, however, a good basic understanding of legal challenges related to cloud and will, I hope, allow you to ask the right questions and make the right decisions to take advantage of this great revolution without putting you and your organization legally at risk.

Sovereignty

There is no ambiguity about Sovereignty. In law, it is defined as the supreme, absolute, and uncontrollable power by which an independent state is governed. As far as cloud is concerned, sovereignty is, therefore, the absolute power over one's data and applications.

Let's get clear from the get-go: using the cloud is accepting loving some power and authority, for, in return, flexibility, performance, and access to innovative services, financially and technologically impossible to get locally.

Let me elaborate! Imagine you decide to outsource your customer relationship management (CRM) application. Application and data are now stored on the servers of your service provider. You so entrust the latter to hardware, backups, and access control management, just to name a few services. You give a portion of your power to your provider in return for a better quality of services, for example, or a universal and fast access.

A few months later, your organization is caught up in a financial scandal and the Prosecutor's office orders access to your customer data stored in the database of your CRM. If the service provider is in the same country as your principal place of business, it's almost indisputable that it will provide access to your data.

What if these data are stored in another country. The Prosecutor's office no longer has sovereignty. So, it will need to go through an international process, which will be more complex, time-consuming and costly. There is, however, a strong chance that he gets it unless he finds himself facing a state in which the law is unclear without legal precedents.

Let's now look at the problem the other way. The Prosecutor's office of the other country launches proceedings against your company. If your data are located in the country of your principal place of business, then we are almost in the previous case and your sovereignty applies. If your data are in the other country, the one who starts the procedure, there are then chances that the law of that country will apply and that access to the data is granted without you and local justice have a say.

The location of the data center is important. Edward Snowden revelations showed that a country like the United States could exercise an abuse of sovereignty and access individuals and company data stored on its soil. Conversely, the appeal won by Microsoft against the Government of the United States indicates that a State may not unilaterally compel a service provider to provide access to data located in another country.

When you read the minutes of the hearing of the case of Microsoft against the Government of the United States[9], you find two particularly interesting points:

- « The effect of the government's demand here impermissibly fell beyond U.S. borders and therefore the Microsoft warrant should be quashed ». In other words, it is not because it is possible to access the data from the United States that the principle of territoriality applies. In this case, the data is stored in Ireland, it's Irish law that applies and the Government of the United States must use the Treaty of mutual judicial assistance, to carry out the mandate on Irish soil. There are several of these treaties, including one with the European Union.
- « The SCA (Stored Communications Act) is outdated and overdue for congressional revision ». This is a crucial point that we meet again later: most of the laws of data protection are no longer in tune with internet

[9] Go to http://www.ca2.uscourts.gov/decisions.html and use docket 14-2985 in the Basic search box

technology. It is urgent to make sure they follow more closely the evolution of the internet.

If one refers to the EU directive 95/46/EC, which regulates data protection in Europe, Parliament has recognized that it no longer met the need of our new digital era. Unlike the United States, for the moment, it was repealed in 2016 and replaced by the Regulation (EU) 2016/679, also called GDPR (*General Data Protection Regulation*)[10]. This regulation is very important for any data stored on the European territory because it gives individuals control over their data and sets standards for the use of data for police and judicial purposes. As it had been pointed out by Marju Lauristin[11], the Member of European Parliament in charge of this case: « In establishing European standards on the exchange of information between law enforcement authorities, the directive on data protection will become a powerful and useful instrument designed to help the authorities to transfer personal data easily and effectively while respecting the fundamental right to privacy ».

This introduces a key point of data storage in the European territory: Community law applies and access to data is governed by regulation 2016/679. Therefore, there is no blank check given to the country in which the data is stored. When you think about it, it seems obvious, and yet, this is not necessarily always the case.

It is interesting to see how this access is interpreted by different providers of cloud services.

- *Microsoft*: Microsoft will not provide any third party: (a) direct, indirect, blanket or unfettered access to Customer Data or Support Data; (b) platform encryption keys used to secure Customer Data or the ability to break such encryption; or (c) access to Customer Data or Support Data if Microsoft is aware that the data is to be used for purposes other than those stated in the third party's request.[12]

---

[10] http://eur-lex.europa.eu/legal-content/en/TXT/?uri=CELEX:32016R0679
[11] http://www.europarl.europa.eu/meps/en/124698/MARJU_LAURISTIN_home.html
[12] https://www.microsoft.com/en-us/Licensing/product-licensing/products.aspx

- *Amazon*: We do not disclose customer content unless we're required to do so to comply with the law or a valid and binding order of a governmental or regulatory body. Governmental and regulatory bodies need to follow the applicable legal process to obtain valid and binding orders.[13]

- *Google*: Google designs its systems to (i) only allow authorized persons to access data they are authorized to access; and (ii) ensure that personal data cannot be read, copied, altered or removed without authorization during processing, use and after recording. The systems are designed to detect any inappropriate access. Google employs a centralized access management system to control personnel access to production servers and only provides access to a limited number of authorized personnel.[14]

- *Dropbox*: Dropbox and its Sub-processors will only process Customer Data to provide the Services and to fulfill Dropbox's obligations under the Agreement. Sub-processors' processing activities will be restricted to processing on Dropbox's behalf and in accordance with Dropbox's instructions. Customer agrees that Dropbox and its Sub-processors may transfer, store, and process Customer Data in locations other than Customer's country.[15]

- *SalesForce.com*: We will maintain administrative, physical, and technical safeguards for the protection of the security, confidentiality, and integrity of Your Data, as described in the Documentation. Those safeguards will include, but will not be limited to, measures for preventing access, use, modification or disclosure of Your Data by Our personnel except (a) to provide the Purchased Services and prevent or address service or technical problems, (b) as compelled by law in accordance with Section 8.3 (Compelled Disclosure) below, or (c) as You expressly permit in writing.[16]

The sovereignty issue seems more complex than it seems at first glance. Yet, while thinking about it deeply and getting back to the definition of sovereignty

---

[13] https://aws.amazon.com/en/compliance/data-privacy-faq/
[14] https://cloud.google.com/terms/data-processing-terms
[15] https://www.dropbox.com/privacy#business_agreement
[16] http://www.salesforce.com/assets/pdf/misc/salesforce_MSA.pdf

as the detention of supreme authority, as soon as your data or applications are hosted by a third party, you abandon your sovereignty. This may shock you, but let's look at the following three possible cases of data storage or application hosting:

1. You own your data center. You have all rights to your data and applications; your sovereignty is absolute.
2. You host data and/or applications at a third party located in the same jurisdiction (the same country or state). You give up your sovereignty to the third party who owns and operates the data center. The service provider is depending on the applicable domestic law, as you are.
3. You host data and/or applications at a third party located in another jurisdiction (another country or state). You abandon your sovereignty to the third party who owns and operates the data center. The latter is not depending on the same applicable law as you are.

If only the first case protects your sovereignty, it is illusory to believe that because the data center is in the same state, its sovereignty is protected. This is, unfortunately, the dupe game which is often exposed by some states who accept the installation of data centers, mainly Chinese ones. If we do often not know the terms of the agreement which binds the provider who finances the data center and the Government, there is a risk of loss of sovereignty as the operator is not the Government itself. The contract, we will see later in this chapter, is so important.

In the case of private companies, one of the questions that remain concerns the dispute and its treatment, more than that of sovereignty. It seems obvious that an international procedure is longer and more expensive than a domestic one. However, the legal framework in the host country is sometimes more complete and favorable to the complainant that in many countries in which laws are not adapted to the digital world. The case of the European GDPR is eloquent and unique, protecting the confidentiality of data more than in any another jurisdiction.

The topic of sovereignty and its loss behind us, let's now have a look at data protection. Who oversees what and what protects it?

Protection

Protecting your data seems like a normal thing. Your bank asks you, for example, not to store your PIN with your credit card. Your customers' data must not be accessible to anyone, including within your own organization. Confidentiality, therefore, plays an important role in the protection of data, but that is not the only reason for protecting them.

The data protection is regulated in the many countries, but not all, by a local legal framework: GDPR in Europe, to which national transpositions exist, such as the Data Protection Act in France and Great Britain. The United States is a special case, as they have a sectoral approach to data protection. As such, they guarantee the protection of personal data through the United States Privacy Act, the Safe Harbor Act and the Health Insurance Portability and Accountability Act. At the same time, they ensure that the government has access in case of national security threats through the Patriot Act. I will return to this topic because it is sensitive since the major providers are North American.

Legal data protection frameworks are in place to respect the principles of fairness, proportionality, information, treatment, and security. It is important to note, however, that if the service provider is required to comply with the law of the jurisdiction in which it operates, its clients will generally be solely responsible to the authorities and the owners of the data they deal with. Outsourcing is therefore by no means a screen behind which customers can hide.

Let us look at five cases of data protection: Europe, the United States, Mauritius, South Africa and the rest of Africa.

Europe

As from 25 May 2018, data protection in Europe is governed by the General Data Protection Regulation[17] (GDPR). One of the key points of this new regulation is that it concerns any organization that offers its services and its goods to the citizens of Europe. Even a Cameroonian company that owns a commercial entity in France is forced to comply with the regulation.

---

[17] The full text can be found here: http://eur-lex.europa.eu/legal-content/EN/TXT/?uri=CELEX:32016R0679

The GDPR can be summed up, but cannot be limited to five main components:

- Increased access rights to their personal data for the EU citizens. We find, among other things, the obligation of explicit and positive consent, as well as the "right to be forgotten". Companies will, therefore, have to obtain the agreement of any person (opt-in) to collect personal data, as well as delete the data of a person who requests it.
- Increased obligations for organizations to secure the data of its customers. One of the basic principles is the by default protection of private data, as soon as the system design. Thus, any information system that manages and stores these data must be "secure".
- An obligation of notification in case of intrusion and data leakage.
- The appointment of a Data Protection Officer for all public and private organizations whose "core activities of the controller or the processor consist of processing operations which, by virtue of their nature, their scope and/or their purposes, require regular and systematic monitoring of data subjects on a large scale". Basically, from the moment you store data from EU citizens for your activities, a person from the organization must be named DPO and act as the primary contact with the control authority.
- Fines in the event of failure to comply. These fines can go up to 20 million euros or 4% of annual global turnover for a commercial company, the highest amount being considered.

Through the GDPR, Europe strengthens both the rights of its citizens, the access security to their data and the mechanisms for controlling such access. As the regulation indicates, from the moment an organization collects data from EU citizens, it must comply with the regulation.

What role can cloud technologies play in all of this? Greater speed of implementation of protection, security and auditing technologies. Indeed, most cloud service providers have already passed through the many security and data access certifications. For example, the standard ISO/IEC 27001 defines the information security management system. Most cloud service providers have their ISO/IEC 27001-certified services. If there is not a perfect match between all the articles and clauses of the GDPR and the ISO/IEC 27011, being certified in accordance with this standard is a big step in the compliance with the GDPR.

De facto, if your information system is not ISO/IEC 27001 certified, you will probably need to go a long way.

The purpose of this book is not to make a comprehensive analysis of cloud services compliance with the GDPR. However, it appears that the use of professional cloud services makes it possible to speed up compliance with the GDPR as well as the implementation of the necessary procedures within the company. A gap analysis should then be done between the different standards in place and the criteria of the GDPR. Depending on the results, you will "only" have to implement procedures and processes required by the information system and the organization. It is highly recommended to use a specialized firm that will accompany the organization in the gap analysis and the implementation of the necessary changes.

The United States

The United States is apart from the rest of the world in many respects. First, most of the major cloud service providers are Americans. Then, the Snowden and Wikileaks affairs amplified the awareness of the possible online espionage of states, starting with that of the United States, the NSA, and the PRISM program. Finally, because the United States do not have a homogeneous legal framework for data protection. They act by industries, both at the federal and state levels.

It is however clear that when talking about cloud services, the specter of the NSA and of the Patriot Act shows up. However, we need to have a look at the Patriot act before talking about data protection.

The Patriot Act

The legislator's imagination has no limit. In the case of the Patriot Act, Patriot is the acronym of *Providing Appropriate Tools Required to Intercept and Obstruct Terrorism*. This is above all a federal law passed as a matter of urgency in 2001 after the tragedy of September 11, to protect the USA from future terrorist attacks.

Without going into the legal details, the Patriot Act authorizes the US government to monitor the digital activities of everyone who is "suspected" of carrying out terrorist activities, whether or not he or she is an American citizen.

However, the law is clear: The Patriot Act does NOT give all the rights to the American government to monitor everyone with impunity.

The latter activities are generally illegal, although sometimes the gap is wide between morality and legality. This means that, legally, if you are hosting data or applications in the United States and your activities are not terrorist, you have nothing to fear, legally. Indeed, if the US government were to suspect you of terrorist activities, a judge would have to issue a search warrant or electronic surveillance for suspicions of terrorism.

So, of course, when you dig a little bit, you realize that the government can request an access called *Sneak and Peek* to "take a look" before notifying the person or organization being targeted. There are, however, jurisprudence and it is unlikely that the government will be allowed such access under the Patriot Act. However, things change radically with the FISA Amendments.

The FISA Amendments

The *Foreign Intelligence Surveillance Act* was voted in 1978 to define the procedures for physical and electronic surveillance (espionage to call a spade a spade). The ACT mainly concerned telephone communications and applied primarily to telephone operators.

In 2008, the Bush administration made amendments to FISA: FISAAA (*Foreign Intelligence Surveillance Act of 1978 Amendments Act of 2008*[18]). In these amendments "the Attorney General and the Director of National Intelligence may authorize jointly, for a period of up to 1 year from the effective date of the authorization, the targeting of persons reasonably believed to be located outside the United States to acquire foreign intelligence information". Follow the restrictions and precautions of use. It should be noted that the supervised person may be a human being, a foreign power, an agent of a foreign power, an officer or an employee of a foreign power, to the principle that it is located outside the United States.

In addition, these amendments broaden the concept of a provider of electronic communications services to providers of "remote computing services", thus cloud service providers! This authorization must follow the procedures of

---

[18] https://www.congress.gov/bill/110th-congress/house-bill/6304/summary/49

94

targeting and limits submitted to the enemy Intelligence Monitoring court, or outside any public legal circuit.

Finally, the service provider must "(A) immediately provide the Government with all information, facilities, or assistance necessary to accomplish the acquisition […], (B) maintain under security procedures approved by the Attorney General and the Director of National Intelligence any records concerning the acquisition or the aid furnished […]."

If you doubted the American government was watching you, thought Edward Snowden was alarmist and took Julian Assange for an activist like many others, well, you were wrong. The US government has the legal arsenal to access any data stored on its soil or on a foreign soil, and in addition to forcing any service provider to help it.

Okay now that you know that Big Brother is watching you, are you going to throw the baby and the bathwater on the pretext that the soap does not froth enough? All the great nations and many small ones have mass monitoring programs. The Americans are undoubtedly the ones who have the most, according to the Wikipedia article on mass surveillance[19]. But, without questioning the role that NSA plays in listening to and decrypting internet communications, storing data in the United States is no riskier, from a point of view of their interception, than to store them on your own servers, provided the systems are connected to the Internet. There is just as much risk that these data will be intercepted by PRISM or Echelon, but much more risk that it is not as safe as in a modernly managed data center. Go back to Chapter 2, Limitations and constraints of the cloud, for more ideas.

Should we be afraid of the Patriot Act and the FISAA? On the principle no, however, we should remain vigilant, as with the access that any government can get, including and especially yours. About the protection of your data, it is, however, necessary to look at Privacy Shield, the successor of Safe Harbor, insofar as this can concern the data stored in Europe.

---

[19] https://en.wikipedia.org/wiki/List_of_government_mass_surveillance_projects

Privacy Shield

Let's start by clarifying an essential point: Privacy Shield replaces Safe Harbor. Now, this is clear, let's have a look at what Privacy Shield is. As we have seen, the United States and Europe do not have the same approach in terms of protecting personal data at all. Where Europe is very "centralized", the United States is organized by business line. Privacy Shield is a set of principles, not a law, issued by the US Department of Commerce to ensure the adequate level of protection of personal data exchanged between Europe and the United States.

This applies to all American companies called upon to process data from its European data centers on the American soil. However, it is important to note that if a national (in Europe), federal or US state law is more restrictive, it is the latter that applies! The same goes, as we have seen, with the GDPR.

So, what does all this bring us? In fact:

- Increased transparency. The companies that manage your data and applications are constrained by the Privacy Shield and must certify that they follow the requirements of transparency and abide by requests for information and cooperation with the European authorities of Data protection.
- Considering the rapid requests for information (45 days maximum) and an arbitration managed by the European authorities.
- A guarantee that the US authorities do not have unlimited access to personal data in an indiscriminate way.

Basically, and to simplify, if your data is stored in Europe, they are protected by the European jurisdiction. Even if it is an American company that treats them, the United States and Europe cooperate to guarantee European rights. This is great news because the specter of Big Brother-NSA-PRISM disappears to give way to EU law.

Once again, however, do not fall into a naive optimism. From the moment a data is broadcasted on the Internet, it is likely to be intercepted by eavesdropping digital ears. However, the existing legal framework shelters abuses if your data is hosted in Europe.

What about the protection of my data in the USA?

The first protection is the one guaranteed by your access provider. For this reason, refer to the service agreement (see page 90) of the latter. However, as noted above, the United States does not have a centralized approach to data protection, so it is necessary to consult the Data Protection Act of your sector of activity. The main ones are the following:

- Health: Health Insurance Portability and Accountability Act (HIPAA)[20]
- Financial services (bank, insurance, fintech, …): Financial Services Modernization Act (Gramm-Leach-Billey Act, GLB)[21], Fair Credit Reporting Act (FCRA), Fair Debt Collection Practices Act (FDCPA)
- Childhood: Children's Online Privacy Protection Act of 1998 (Coppa)[22]

Depending on the data you are storing, there is a strong bet that your cloud provider will be certified to comply with one of the laws below. Just go to the websites of the main service providers to discover their many certifications:

- Microsoft: https://www.microsoft.com/en-us/trustcenter/compliance/complianceofferings
- Amazon: https://aws.amazon.com/compliance/
- Google: https://cloud.google.com/security/compliance
- Salesforce: https://trust.salesforce.com/en/compliance/

Of course, this does not give free hand to all the customers. The laws in force regarding the data collected, the information provided to the clients, the right of access, the length of retention, the use it makes,… should be respected.

In conclusion about the data stored on the American territory, it can be said that they are protected. They are certainly not immune to their seizure or interception by the US government, particularly in the context of the FISAAA, but if you do not have suspicious activities, there is little risk. In any case, less risk than those taken by storing them in a local data center that does not necessarily meet international norms and standards.

---

[20] http://www.hhs.gov/ocr/hipaa/
[21] http://legislink.org/us/pl-106-102
[22] http://legislink.org/us/pl-105-277

Mauritius

Mauritius is the small economic miracle of the Indian Ocean. It was one of the first African countries to adopt a Data Protection Act on December 27, 2004. 13 years later, Mauritius enacted its new Data Protection Act on December 22, 2017. It is interesting to take a closer look at the data protection approach described in this act.

The six principles of data protection of the Republic of Mauritius are described on the DPO website (*Data Protection Office*)[23] :

- *Lawfulness, fairness, and transparency*. The principle of legal, fair and transparent treatment of personal data.
- *Purpose specification*. The data must be collected for explicit, specified and legitimate purposes and not further processed in a manner incompatible with those purposes.
- *Adequacy, relevance, and limitation*. Personal data should be adequate, relevant and limited to what is necessary in relation to the purposes for which they are processed.
- *Accuracy and up-to-date*. The data must be accurate and where necessary, kept up to date, with every reasonable step being taken to ensure that any inaccurate personal data are erased or rectified without delay.
- *Time limitation*. The data should be kept in a form which permits identification of data subjects for no longer than is necessary for the purposes for which the personal data are processed.
- *Respect for data subject rights*. The data is processed in accordance with the rights of the of data subjects.

It's interesting to note that two principles that were part of the 2004 act have been set aside: *Security and control over transborder data flows*. This does not mean that those have disappeared from the law but are now embedded into the others.

The principle of transborder data flows is important since it allows the use of public cloud. However, article 36 of the 2017 act expands article 31 of the 2004

---

[23] http://dataprotection.govmu.org/English/Legislation/Pages/Principles-relating-to-personal-data.aspx

act. It starts with the fact that personal data may transfer personal data to another country, provided that the controller or processor has provided to the Commissioner of the *Data Protection Office* the proof that data is protected, and that the data subject has provided consent (which aligns with GDPR). Of course, the transfer need to be necessary and legal.

The concept of data Controller, that is, the natural or legal person who recovers and uses the personal data, will be noticed in the law. Part IV of the Act defines the obligations of the data controller in terms of collection, information, access, use, audit, and data security. It should be noted that the right to be forgotten is foreseen and that any person may request the destruction of the data concerning her.

What about state interference in unconditional access to personal data? It is quite clear and authorized by the Prime Minister for matters of national security. This is the objective of article 44. It is sufficient for the Prime Minister to unilaterally decide that to preserve national safety the *Data Protection Act 2017* does not apply, for the government to have unconditional access to the necessary data. To this day there is not, to my knowledge, jurisprudence on this matter.

It can, therefore, be concluded that from the point of view of the protection of personal data in Mauritius, the *Data Protection Act 2017* is properly framed in such a way as to protect individuals from the processing of their personal data, whether they are stored in Mauritius or in another jurisdiction. It is, however, worth noting that for any *Data Controller or processor* having an establishment in Mauritius, even an "innocuous" operation such as the use of cookies must be the subject of a declaration to the *Data Protection Office*, must be accepted by the user after being informed and must comply with the *Data Protection Act 2017*. The collection of information by the search engines is also concerned.

South Africa

The first African country in terms of GDP is often looked at and taken as an example of economic development. What about data protection? The personal data protection act is relatively recent since it dates from November 26, 2013. The *Protection of Personal Information Act No. 4*[24], or PoPI, sets out the legal

---

[24] http://www.justice.gov.za/legislation/acts/2013-004.pdf

and legal framework for the collection and processing of personal data, the latter applying to natural and legal persons (legal persons).

PoPI defines the legal framework with eight main conditions:

- *Accountability*. The *"Responsible parties"*, that is, the natural or legal persons collecting and processing the data are responsible before the law for the respect of PoPI.
- *Processing limitation*. The data can only be processed legally, for the stated purpose, with the consent of the person concerned. These data must be adequate, relevant and sufficient. The right to be forgotten applies.
- *Purpose specification*. The data can only be collected and processed in the context of a legal and declared objective. They should be kept only for a limited time to the pursuit of the stated objective. The deletion of the data should not allow rebuilding it later.
- *Further processing limitation*. The data can be processed for an additional purpose provided that it is compatible with the previous objective.
- *Information quality*. The necessary steps are in place to ensure that the data are complete, precise, accurate and updated.
- *Openness*. The treatments must be documented. The subjects of this data must be informed, as well as the identity of the natural or legal person using this data. The subjects must also be informed of the obligatory or voluntary nature of the data collection, the consequences in case of refusal, the transfer of data outside the South African jurisdiction or a third party and the rights of the subject.
- *Security safeguards*. The natural or legal person processing the data must take all appropriate and reasonable technical and organizational measures to ensure the security and confidentiality of the data in its possession. It must also inform the regulator and the persons concerned in the event of theft or data leakage.
- *Data subject participation*. Any subject has the right to access, modify or delete the data concerning it.

PoPI makes a distinction between personal data and special personal data. This is the focus of Part B of PoPI. This special information concerns religious or philosophical beliefs, race and ethnic origin, union membership, political opinions, health or sex life, biometric information, criminal records and all the information about the children.

The collection and processing of such data are prohibited, except for organizations whose object is one of the above. For example, a trade union organization may be allowed to collect information about its members, collecting, in fact, their union membership. The same goes for churches or political parties.

In the case of health information by organizations such as hospitals or insurance, the collection, and processing of such information should be linked directly to the services provided, as, for instance, the assessment of diagnostics or risk. In all cases, professional secrecy applies and takes precedence over the sharing of this information.

The Data Protection Authority (*Information Regulator*), also called the regulator, oversees promoting and enforcing PoPI. Any collection and processing of personal data must be declared to the regulator. If it is in charge of the application of the eight principles of data protection and the protection of individuals whose data are collected, it defines the parameters of the international data exchange.

Cross-border exchange

At the time of writing this book, IBM has a data center in South Africa, Microsoft is about to open two, and Amazon has expressed interest in opening one. If there are some local public cloud vendors, a large part of the data collected and processed is outside of the South African jurisdiction. Chapter 9 of PoPI defines its principles.

By default, PoPI prohibits the exchange of data beyond the borders of South Africa, unless the following conditions are met:

- The legal framework for data protection is "substantially" like that of South Africa, as described by PoPI;
- The subject consents to the transfer;
- The transfer is necessary to the processing or the performance of the data processing;

- The transfer is for the benefit of the subject.

Basically, if the legal framework is adequate, the subject agrees, and the benefits are there, everything is fine. This opens the door to the public cloud without the need to make any additional statement to the regulator. But there are three things to note that are important for the choice of the use of a public cloud:

1- The storage jurisdiction must be known since its legal framework must be compatible with that of South Africa;
2- The regulator may recommend blocking a provider if the protection rules are not compatible with those of PoPI. It may therefore also recommend blocking the storage of information in a country;
3- The subject must consent to the transfer.

This last point seems to be particularly restrictive because it is not only about informing the subject but of obtaining its consent. There is, therefore, a strong bet that the transfer clause will appear in the general conditions of data collection and that the subject is therefore not really aware since it will have accepted the general conditions without reading them ...

In conclusion, with PoPI, South Africa describes its data protection framework in a relatively comprehensive manner. As many countries however technology advances faster than legislation, and, for example, PoPI does not define specific restrictions on cookies or the collection of the user's location. This information falls within the general framework of PoPI, must have general conditions aligned with PoPI and be the subject of a declaration by the entity collecting this data.

Let's now look at the overall picture of the other African countries.

The rest of Africa

On 27 June 2014, the African Union adopted the Convention on Cyber Security and Personal Data Protection by the 53 African signatory countries. If this Convention does not have the force of a law, it defines a framework that puts the protection of personal data at the forefront. To date, some 30 countries, including the strong economies that are Nigeria, Kenya, and Ethiopia, have put in place a data protection law, generally modeled on that of Europe's Directive

95/46/EC, and more and more in the future on GDPR for questions of pure simplification and alignment.

In most cases, the concepts of personal data and sensitive data, regulator, and reporting, responsibilities, and obligations, and cross-border control are found. So, all the legal frameworks are similar, which is not surprising. However, I advise you to consult your legal adviser before embarking on any public cloud project.

If we have seen that hosting data with a third party is an immediate loss of sovereignty, it is not the case with the need to protect individuals, by respecting the law. Not complying with the law can have hefty consequences: Up to 10 years in prison in South Africa, 2 years in Mauritius and 4% of the global turnover of the company in Europe. Something to think about!

Now that we have a better understanding of the framework for the protection of personal data, let's look at what the security is and who is responsible for what in the event of a failure.

Security

As soon as we talk about cloud, security comes as one of the first three areas of concern. We have encountered it in the previous chapters and will find it again in the following. In these times of cyber attacks, manipulation of elections and *Dark web*, security is in every mind.

What does the law provide in terms of data security, treatment, and access? Whatever law we look at, the least we can say is that it's not prescriptive. Take the GDPR, sections 32 to 34 define the safety rules to be followed and the notification and communication procedures in case of breach of security and breach of personal data.

Section 2 requires that *"the controller and the processor shall implement appropriate technical and organizational measures to ensure a level of security appropriate to the risk"*. There is two important information in this sentence:

- Security is not only the cloud provider concern (the processor), it is also that of the controller (the person who collects and processes the data). The cloud provider can, therefore, implement all the necessary technical, physical or logical means, if the controller does not have the processes and procedures in place to secure the data and the treatment, he fails to his obligations. The regulatory framework has also provided that the establishment of a code of conduct (article 40) and a certification mechanism (article 42) is a means of demonstrating " Compliance with the requirements ».

- Security must be adapted to the risk. It may seem obvious. It makes it necessary to find a precarious balance between law and cost, and therefore to make lawyers and computer scientists speak in order to fully understand the issues of data collection and processing.

The four aspects to be implemented to ensure data security are noted in article 32:

1- Data encryption and pseudonymization;
2- The technical means to ensure "the confidentiality, integrity, availability and resilience" of information processing systems and services. Note that it is not a matter of physical or logical systems, but also of procedures and processes, in which humans play an important role;
3- The means of restoring systems in the event of a failure, whether it is physical (e.g. physical destruction of the data center) or technical (e.g. erasing, encrypting or moving data);
4- Procedures to test the strength of the system and the organization.

The path of the safety standards is quickly found and, the ISO K series which defines the framework of a secured information system.

In the event of failure and data breach, it is necessary to declare it to the competent supervisory authority and to the concerned people, irrespective of the fact the breach comes from the processor or the controller. It is, however, interesting to note that under the GDPR, this obligation to communicate to the concerned persons may not be necessary if, for example, the data are anonymized and encrypted, thus unusable by unauthorized third parties. In any case, the control authority must be notified.

These measures and actions are found in all the legal frameworks of the countries that have implemented a law to protect personal data.

So, we see that the legislator has taken into account the concept of cloud security and put it in the hands of both the provider and the data controller. As we have already seen, security is everyone's business. It is not complex when you apply a bit of common sense and a good dose of discipline. Adherence to standards forms an indispensable first layer, so the use of already certified public cloud providers is an indisputable precondition. The second layer concerns adherence to the standards of one's own information system. The third layer concerns the procedures and processes put in place by the organization to reduce the risk of loss of information to a minimum, especially at the level of individuals using biometric processes and rights management on documents and data.

If the use of a secure public cloud helps to protect its data and its processing, it does not remove the obligations of the controller. The wrongs can be shared, as they can be dependent solely on the controller. The bank cannot be held liable if you have not locked your safe after filling it.

We see that the responsibilities in terms of security have been anticipated by the legislator. What about the privacy of the data and their access, and the damage caused in case of intrusion on their systems? That's what we're going to see now.

Privacy

Security, protection, and privacy are intimately linked. In fact, the legal frameworks on data protection define the safety rules to be applied to data, applications, and access in order to guarantee the confidentiality of personal data stored and manipulated by the service provider.

All providers guarantee the privacy of the data, of course, their commercial credibility is at stake. Let's look at how, for the main market players, as we have done for data sovereignty:

- *Microsoft*: "Customer Data will be used only to provide Customer the Online Services including purposes compatible with providing those services. Microsoft will not use Customer Data or derive information from it for any advertising or similar commercial purposes. As between the parties, Customer retains all right, title and interest in and to

Customer Data. Microsoft acquires no rights in Customer Data, other than the rights Customer grants to Microsoft to provide the Online Services to Customer".

"Microsoft will not disclose Customer Data or Support Data outside of Microsoft or its controlled subsidiaries and affiliates except (1) as Customer directs, (2) as described in the OST, or (3) as required by law. Microsoft is committed to helping protect the security of Customer's information. Microsoft has implemented and will maintain and follow appropriate technical and organizational measures intended to protect Customer Data and Support Data against accidental, unauthorized or unlawful access, disclosure, alteration, loss, or destruction". [25]

- *Amazon*: "At AWS, Customers maintain ownership of their customer content and select which AWS services process, store and host their customer content. We do not access or use customer content for any purpose without the customer's consent. We never use customer content or derive information from it for marketing or advertising".

  "Customers choose how their customer content is secured. We offer our customers strong encryption for customer content in transit or at rest, and we provide customers with the option to manage their own encryption keys".

  "We have developed a security assurance program using global privacy and data protection best practices in order to help customers establish, operate and leverage our security control environment. These security protections and control processes are independently validated by multiple third-party independent assessments". [26]

- *Google*: "Google will implement and maintain technical and organizational measures to protect Customer Data against accidental or unlawful destruction, loss, alteration, unauthorized disclosure or access". [27] It should be noted that apart from adherence to the standards, such as ISO/IEC 27018, and the paragraphs on data

---

[25] https://www.microsoft.com/en-us/licensing/product-licensing/products.aspx, pick Online Services Terms (OST)

[26] https://aws.amazon.com/compliance/data-privacy-faq/

[27] Https://cloud.google.com/terms/data-processing-terms

protection that I put forward on page 89, no reference to the protection of the confidentiality of the data is described.

- *Dropbox*: "Our Services are designed to make it simple for you to store Your Stuff, collaborate with others, and work across multiple devices. To make that possible, we store, process, and transmit Your Stuff—like files, messages, comments, and photos—as well as information related to it".

  "We may share information as discussed below, but we won't sell it to advertisers or other third parties (the "share" described covers third-party companies, other users, and applications, as well as administrators in the context of enterprise contracts)".

  "We may disclose your information to third parties if we determine that such disclosure is reasonably necessary to (a) comply with the law; (b) protect any person from death or serious bodily injury; (c) prevent fraud or abuse of Dropbox or our users; or (d) protect Dropbox's property rights"[28]

- *SalesForce.com*: ""Confidential Information" means all information disclosed by a party ("Disclosing Party") to the other party ("Receiving Party"), whether orally or in writing, that is designated as confidential or that reasonably should be understood to be confidential given the nature of the information and the circumstances of disclosure".

  "The Receiving Party will use the same degree of care that it uses to protect the confidentiality of its own confidential information".

  "The Receiving Party may disclose Confidential Information of the Disclosing Party to the extent compelled by law to do so, provided the Receiving Party gives the Disclosing Party prior notice of the compelled disclosure (to the extent legally permitted) and reasonable assistance, at the Disclosing Party's cost, if the Disclosing Party wishes to contest the disclosure".[29]

You see by reading the terms and conditions of the different providers above that the notion of data confidentiality is globally treated poorly, apart from Microsoft which also defines the notion of ownership of data stored by its

---

[28] https://www.dropbox.com/privacy
[29] Http://www.salesforce.com/assets/pdf/misc/salesforce_MSA.pdf

Services. The most worrying provider here is Google who, while trying to reassure on data security, provides no information on confidentiality of data stored on its servers and neither on the use that the company does. Google is known to practice the "opt-out", meaning that anything you do not explicitly request is allowed. As a result, stored data can be used, for example, to better adapt the search engine to ad targeting. A clear breach of data privacy in my opinion.

It can, therefore, be estimated that as for the sovereignty of the data, storing information in the cloud means to partially abandon privacy. Is that bad news? When you look at it a little closer, not necessarily for the following reasons:

1. Most service providers secure data in a way that is generally superior to what we could do. Note the mentions of Microsoft and Amazon about their security practices.
2. In the event of a breach of security and data leakage, these providers are required to declare it by their adherence to the standards. An obvious benefit for customers who will have to be immediately informed of any data leakage.
3. As a rule, compliance with standards and the implementation of good security and privacy practices of these providers force customers to implement their processes and procedures to directly benefit their Customers. It should be noted that by 2018 for companies dealing with Europe, the sanctions related to GDPR will force compliance and overall increase the processing of data privacy.

As for the security or the sovereignty of the data, outsourcing the storage and processing of these data and those of its customers is a global good news for their confidentiality. The responsibility for the damage caused in case of data leakage remains to be defined. What about the responsibility of the service provider or his direct client? In other words, if my data stored in a cloud service provider by one of my vendors (for example, my bank or my insurance company) is hacked and I am harmed (for example, by diverting a sum of money from my account), who carries the responsibility of paying me back?

Let's imagine a cloud service provider that runs not a hundred merchant sites, but several hundreds of thousands, some thousands of which generate millions of dollars in revenue per month. Can this provider repay all of his clients' lost income in the event of an accidental failure? The answer is probably no unless you want to bankrupt it automatically. As a result, the entire profession will limit liabilities. Before we look at the details, let us take the problem from another angle and imagine that the few thousand merchant sites are each hosted on infrastructure owned by the companies that own the sites. If each site were to stop for a hardware failure problem, would the owner turn to the hardware manufacturer, software developer or network provider who implemented the site? If this could be possible, there is a strong bet that it will not be because each of these companies will have in its terms and conditions a limited liability. This is the same for cloud service providers. Let's look at the response of some of these providers:

- *Microsoft*. "To the extent permitted by applicable law, each party's total liability for all claims relating to Professional Services will be limited to the amounts Customer was required to pay for the Professional Services or the limitation of liability for the Online Service with which the Professional Services are offered, whichever is greater. In no event will either party be liable for indirect, incidental, special, punitive, or consequential damages, including loss of use, loss of profits, or interruption of business, however, caused or on any theory of liability in relation to the Professional Services". [30]

- *Amazon*. "WE AND OUR AFFILIATES AND LICENSORS WILL NOT BE LIABLE TO YOU FOR ANY DIRECT, INDIRECT, INCIDENTAL, SPECIAL, CONSEQUENTIAL OR EXEMPLARY DAMAGES (INCLUDING DAMAGES FOR LOSS OF PROFITS, REVENUES, CUSTOMERS, OPPORTUNITIES, GOODWILL, USE, OR DATA), EVEN IF A PARTY HAS BEEN ADVISED OF THE POSSIBILITY OF SUCH DAMAGES. FURTHER, NEITHER WE NOR ANY OF OUR AFFILIATES OR LICENSORS WILL BE RESPONSIBLE FOR ANY COMPENSATION, REIMBURSEMENT, OR DAMAGES ARISING IN CONNECTION WITH: (A) YOUR INABILITY TO USE THE SERVICES, INCLUDING AS A RESULT OF ANY (I) TERMINATION OR SUSPENSION OF THIS AGREEMENT OR YOUR USE OF OR ACCESS TO THE SERVICE OFFERINGS, (II) OUR DISCONTINUATION OF ANY OR ALL OF THE

---

[30] https://www.microsoft.com/en-us/licensing/product-licensing/products.aspx, pick Online Services Terms (OST)

SERVICE OFFERINGS, OR, (III) WITHOUT LIMITING ANY OBLIGATIONS UNDER THE SERVICE LEVEL AGREEMENTS, ANY UNANTICIPATED OR UNSCHEDULED DOWNTIME OF ALL OR A PORTION OF THE SERVICES FOR ANY REASON; (B) THE COST OF PROCUREMENT OF SUBSTITUTE GOODS OR SERVICES; (C) ANY INVESTMENTS, EXPENDITURES, OR COMMITMENTS BY YOU IN CONNECTION WITH THIS AGREEMENT OR YOUR USE OF OR ACCESS TO THE SERVICE OFFERINGS; OR (D) ANY UNAUTHORIZED ACCESS TO, ALTERATION OF, OR THE DELETION, DESTRUCTION, DAMAGE, LOSS OR FAILURE TO STORE ANY OF YOUR CONTENT OR OTHER DATA. IN ANY CASE, EXCEPT FOR PAYMENT OBLIGATIONS UNDER SECTION 9.2, OUR AND OUR AFFILIATES' AND LICENSORS' AGGREGATE LIABILITY UNDER THIS AGREEMENT WILL NOT EXCEED THE AMOUNT YOU ACTUALLY PAY US UNDER THIS AGREEMENT FOR THE SERVICE THAT GAVE RISE TO THE CLAIM DURING THE 12 MONTHS BEFORE THE LIABILITY AROSE".[31]

We have retained the capital letters to the extent that this article appears in capital letters on the AWS site. It should be noted that articles 10 (disclaimer) and 11 (Limitations of liability) are the only ones to be in full capital! A way to draw attention to their importance probably.

- *Google*. "13.1 Limitation on Indirect Liability. TO THE MAXIMUM EXTENT PERMITTED BY APPLICABLE LAW, NEITHER PARTY, NOR GOOGLE'S SUPPLIERS, WILL BE LIABLE UNDER THIS AGREEMENT FOR LOST REVENUES OR INDIRECT, SPECIAL, INCIDENTAL, CONSEQUENTIAL, EXEMPLARY, OR PUNITIVE DAMAGES, EVEN IF THE PARTY KNEW OR SHOULD HAVE KNOWN THAT SUCH DAMAGES WERE POSSIBLE AND EVEN IF DIRECT DAMAGES DO NOT SATISFY A REMEDY".

"13.2 Limitation on Amount of Liability. TO THE MAXIMUM EXTENT PERMITTED BY APPLICABLE LAW, NEITHER PARTY, NOR GOOGLE'S SUPPLIERS, MAY BE HELD LIABLE UNDER THIS AGREEMENT FOR MORE THAN THE AMOUNT PAID BY CUSTOMER TO GOOGLE UNDER THIS AGREEMENT DURING THE TWELVE MONTHS PRIOR TO THE EVENT GIVING RISE TO LIABILITY".[32]

---

[31] https://aws.amazon.com/agreement/
[32] https://cloud.google.com/terms/

- *Dropbox.* "WE DON'T EXCLUDE OR LIMIT OUR LIABILITY TO YOU WHERE IT WOULD BE ILLEGAL TO DO SO—THIS INCLUDES ANY LIABILITY FOR DROPBOX'S OR ITS AFFILIATES' FRAUD OR FRAUDULENT MISREPRESENTATION IN PROVIDING THE SERVICES. IN COUNTRIES WHERE THE FOLLOWING TYPES OF EXCLUSIONS AREN'T ALLOWED, WE'RE RESPONSIBLE TO YOU ONLY FOR LOSSES AND DAMAGES THAT ARE A REASONABLY FORESEEABLE RESULT OF OUR FAILURE TO USE REASONABLE CARE AND SKILL OR OUR BREACH OF OUR CONTRACT WITH YOU. THIS PARAGRAPH DOESN'T AFFECT CONSUMER RIGHTS THAT CAN'T BE WAIVED OR LIMITED BY ANY CONTRACT OR AGREEMENT.

  IN COUNTRIES WHERE EXCLUSIONS OR LIMITATIONS OF LIABILITY ARE ALLOWED, DROPBOX, ITS AFFILIATES, SUPPLIERS OR DISTRIBUTORS WON'T BE LIABLE FOR:

  i. ANY INDIRECT, SPECIAL, INCIDENTAL, PUNITIVE, EXEMPLARY OR CONSEQUENTIAL DAMAGES, OR

  ii. ANY LOSS OF USE, DATA, BUSINESS, OR PROFITS, REGARDLESS OF LEGAL THEORY.

  THESE EXCLUSIONS OR LIMITATIONS WILL APPLY REGARDLESS OF WHETHER OR NOT DROPBOX OR ANY OF ITS AFFILIATES HAS BEEN WARNED OF THE POSSIBILITY OF SUCH DAMAGES.

  IF YOU USE THE SERVICES FOR ANY COMMERCIAL, BUSINESS OR RE-SALE PURPOSE, DROPBOX, ITS AFFILIATES, SUPPLIERS OR DISTRIBUTORS WILL HAVE NO LIABILITY TO YOU FOR ANY LOSS OF PROFIT, LOSS OF BUSINESS, BUSINESS INTERRUPTION, OR LOSS OF BUSINESS OPPORTUNITY. DROPBOX AND ITS AFFILIATES AREN'T RESPONSIBLE FOR THE CONDUCT, WHETHER ONLINE OR OFFLINE, OF ANY USER OF THE SERVICES.

  OTHER THAN FOR THE TYPES OF LIABILITY WE CANNOT LIMIT BY LAW (AS DESCRIBED IN THIS SECTION), WE LIMIT OUR LIABILITY TO YOU TO THE GREATER OF $20 USD OR 100% OF ANY AMOUNT YOU'VE PAID UNDER YOUR CURRENT SERVICE PLAN WITH DROPBOX".[33]

- *SalesForce.com.* "EXCEPT WHERE PROHIBITED, THE SERVICES ENTITIES SHALL NOT BE LIABLE FOR ANY INDIRECT, SPECIAL, INCIDENTAL,

---

[33] https://www.dropbox.com/terms

CONSEQUENTIAL, OR EXEMPLARY DAMAGES ARISING FROM YOUR USE OF THE SITES OR ANY THIRD PARTY'S USE OF THE SITES. THESE EXCLUSIONS INCLUDE, WITHOUT LIMITATION, DAMAGES FOR LOST PROFITS, LOST DATA, COMPUTER FAILURE, OR THE VIOLATION OF YOUR RIGHTS BY ANY THIRD PARTY, EVEN IF THE SERVICES ENTITIES HAVE BEEN ADVISED OF THE POSSIBILITY THEREOF AND REGARDLESS OF THE LEGAL OR EQUITABLE THEORY UPON WHICH THE CLAIM IS BASED".[34]

It seems that as soon as it comes to responsibility and liability, capital letters become the standard!

I think that the articles coming from the terms and conditions of different providers are eloquent. At best, you can be repaid the amount of your annual subscription, regardless of the damage caused.

Is it necessary to throw the baby and the bathwater? As I stated before, probably not. There are many ways to protect yourself, and these providers propose all of them. From redundancy to data encryption, the technical solutions exist. It comes down to weigh risks and costs, an equation you're your CFO will know, but that they sometimes do not consider. As we tend to say, cheap can be expensive. You must decide accordingly!

Last but one stop on our legal journey: intellectual property. If the industry agrees on the ownership of your data, what really is the intellectual property and especially the responsibility in case of infringement? This is what we look at in the next section

Intellectual Property

As I have already indicated, it is now agreed to leave full ownership of the data stored to the customers. Writing this, I suggest that there was a time when this was not the case. Unfortunately, it is not a misunderstanding, since a few years back, Google assumed the rights to the data stored on its services, allowing itself

---

[34] https://www.salesforce.com/company/legal/sfdc-website-terms-of-service.jsp

to use the content to create its own works. This time is fortunately gone, as this article indicates of their terms of service:

"Except as expressly set forth in this Agreement, this Agreement does not grant either party any rights, implied or otherwise, to the other's content or any of the other's intellectual property. As between the parties, Customer owns all Intellectual Property Rights in Customer Data and the Application or Project (if applicable), and Google owns all Intellectual Property Rights in the Services and Software".

That has the merit of being clear. The same goes for all the other service providers. Data, files, and applications stored and executed on the service provider's servers belong exclusively to the client, and as a result, the service provider cannot exercise any rights to it.

By storing customer data, the service provider indicates in the terms and conditions that it retains the right to access and read this data in order to provide services to the customer. For example, consider the "Use of Customer Data" clause in Microsoft's online service terms:

"Customer Data will be used only to provide Customer the Online Services including purposes compatible with providing those services. Microsoft will not use Customer Data or derive information from it for any advertising or similar commercial purposes. As between the parties, Customer retains all right, title and interest in and to Customer Data. Microsoft acquires no rights in Customer Data, other than the rights Customer grants to Microsoft to provide the Online Services to Customer. This paragraph does not affect Microsoft's rights in software or services Microsoft licenses to Customer."

The first sentence of this clause does not suffer any ambiguity: Microsoft uses your data to provide online services. What are these uses, are we then entitled to ask? As a rule, these are indexing, anti-malware or analysis services. For example, e-mail messages are indexed to be able to speed up searches. In order to be able to create this index, you should be able to read the content of the messages. Another example concerns the protection of attachments. Their content will be analyzed to verify that they do not contain viruses or other malware. Again, the documents are made to protect the end user.

Of this rule and the respect of the ownership of the data by the service provider derive that of respect for intellectual property. Once again, the service provider limits its liability since it could not be held responsible if one of its clients violated the intellectual property of a third party. In other words, if one of its customer's stores data or applications that do not belong to her, it is the client who is one hundred percent responsible for this intellectual property violation, as indicated for example in the "Acceptable Use Policy" clause of Microsoft's online service terms:

"Neither Customer, nor those that access an Online Service through Customer, may use an Online Service:

- to violate the rights of others; […]

Violation of the terms in this section may result in suspension of the Online Service. Microsoft will suspend the Online Service only to the extent reasonably necessary. Unless Microsoft believes an immediate suspension is required, Microsoft will provide reasonable notice before suspending an Online Service".

To conclude this part about intellectual property, it can, therefore, be said that the intellectual property of the client is protected by the service provider, as well as that of others. The service provider stores and processes these data and applications in accordance with the terms of service and enforces the right of others where appropriate.

But where and how to enforce this right? That's what we're going to see now.

Agreement and applicable law

By starting the use of cloud services, you have, implicitly or explicitly, accepted the terms of the online services that the provider generally makes available on its site. The previous sections of this chapter referred to it for a few vendors. Generally, the provider will provide these general conditions upon request, if they are not available directly.

The first aspect that can complicate the relationship between the customer and the service provider concerns the jurisdiction. Here are some examples:

- *Microsoft*. Clause 9 of Attachment 3 of the Online Services Terms: "The Clauses shall be governed by the law of the Member State in which the data exporter is established". [35]
  It should be noted that in this case, the data exporter is the one transferring them, that is the customer. However, this clause complies with the European law and will evolve to be aligned with the GDPR. Meanwhile for any customer located outside the European Union's borders, and storing its data in the EU, the data importer is Microsoft Ireland Operations Limited, and Irish law applies.
- *Amazon Web Services*. Clause 13.4 of the AWS Customer Agreement: "The laws of the State of Washington, without reference to conflict of law rules, govern this Agreement and any dispute of any sort that might arise between you and us. The United Nations Convention for the International Sale of Goods does not apply to this Agreement".[36]
- *Google*. Clause 16.10 of the Terms of Service: " ALL CLAIMS ARISING OUT OF OR RELATING TO THIS AGREEMENT OR THE SERVICES WILL BE GOVERNED BY CALIFORNIA LAW, EXCLUDING THAT STATE'S CONFLICT OF LAWS RULES, AND WILL BE LITIGATED EXCLUSIVELY IN THE FEDERAL OR STATE COURTS OF SANTA CLARA COUNTY, CALIFORNIA, USA; THE PARTIES CONSENT TO PERSONAL JURISDICTION IN THOSE COURTS".[37]
  The capital letters appear as such on the Google site.
- *Dropbox*. Clause 12.4 of the Business Agreement: "THE AGREEMENT WILL BE GOVERNED BY CALIFORNIA LAW EXCEPT FOR ITS CONFLICTS OF LAWS PRINCIPLES".[38]
- *SalesForce.com*. "These Terms are governed by and construed in accordance with the laws of California, without regard to its conflict of laws rules. You expressly agree that the exclusive jurisdiction for any claim or dispute under these Terms and or your use of the Services resides in the courts located in San Francisco, California, and you further

---

[35] https://www.microsoft.com/en-us/licensing/product-licensing/products.aspx, pick Online Services Terms (OST)
[36] https://aws.amazon.com/agreement/
[37] https://cloud.google.com/terms/
[38] https://www.dropbox.com/privacy#business_agreement

expressly agree to submit to the personal jurisdiction of such courts for litigating any such claim or action".[39]

The above examples are all from American companies. If we look at the terms and conditions of French companies like Orange Business Services, for example, the applicable jurisdiction will be France. For Rackspace, a British company, it is the courts of England and Wales which are sovereign. Deutsche Telekom and its Open Telekom Cloud service are governed by German law. The question of jurisdiction can, therefore, be an important point in the choice of the provider. However, it is also appropriate to read between the lines, especially for large access providers such as Microsoft or Amazon Web services, since not all Services are always available in the country of origin of the contract.

Figure 4-1 - Microsoft Azure Regions in December 2017

Amazon is a bit of a case because the jurisdiction is that of the state of Washington, where local and federal law applies. Microsoft, on the other hand, can be a more difficult, particularly if you use Azure. Microsoft seamlessly

---

[39] https://www.salesforce.com/company/legal/sfdc-website-terms-of-service.jsp

provides the list of Azure regions on its site at https://azure.microsoft.com/en-us/regions/.

However, on the screen copy shown on Figure 4-1 - Microsoft Azure Regions in December 2017, notice the *Explore products per region* button. By clicking on it you can see the availability of services by region. For example, very few artificial Intelligence services are available in Europe, as shown in a partial view of the table of AI services illustrated in Figure 4-2 - Availability of Azure services by region.

Products	NON-REGIONAL*	NORTH EUROPE	WEST EUROPE	GERMANY NON-REGIONAL*	GERMANY CENTRAL	GERMANY NORTHEAST	UK WEST	UK SOUTH
AI + Cognitive Services								
Machine Learning Studio			●		●			
Machine Learning Services								
Machine Learning Experimentation Service								
Machine Learning Model Management								
Azure Bot Service		●	●					
Cognitive Services								
Academic Knowledge API								
Bing Autosuggest API	●							
Bing Custom Search API	●							
Bing Image Search API	●							
Bing News Search API	●							

Figure 4-2 - Availability of Azure services by region

So imagine that from a technical point of view, you are storing your data in Ireland, and your applications are using AI services that are only available in the United States, as indicated on Figure 4-3 - . If the West US data center fails, your application is likely to fail too, without Microsoft Ireland Operation LTD being there for anything. A legal imbroglio is likely to happen if you decide to take legal action against the provider with whom you signed the contract, while the one who provides the service is in another jurisdiction.

Products	NON-REGIONAL*	EAST US	EAST US 2	CENTRAL US	NORTH CENTRAL US	SOUTH CENTRAL US	WEST CENTRAL US	WEST US	WEST US 2
AI + Cognitive Services									
Machine Learning Studio		●				●	●		
Machine Learning Services		●					●		
Machine Learning Experimentation Service		●					●		
Machine Learning Model Management		●					●		
Azure Bot Service		●	●	●	●			●	●
Cognitive Services								●	
Academic Knowledge API								●	
Bing Autosuggest API	●								
Bing Custom Search API	●								
Bing Image Search API	●								

Figure 4-3 - Availability of the Azure artificial Intelligence services

This scenario, which may seem a bit far-fetched, will, however, become commonplace. It is technically difficult and sometimes unjustified economically for Microsoft to deploy all of its services across all of the Azure regions. Google says it is impossible to know at any given time where customer's data is located because, for optimization questions, this data can be spread over a data center set as close to the users as possible. Cosmos DB (Microsoft), Dynamo DB (Amazon), or Mongo DB databases are designed to distribute their data across multiple servers available in multiple data centers to minimize the latency of applications that connect to them. The data is then replicated in real time in several data centers, located in different countries and different jurisdictions.

By touching the complexity of the cloud, we understand that laws and behaviors must adapt. However, this adaptation is now infinitely slower than the development of cloud technologies and that of the networking of services around the planet.

When it is only your rights against a service provider, we have seen that the agreement that binds you is relatively well structured, although interpretation and jurisprudence will undoubtedly evolve in the years to come. But what happens in case of business closure, stop or transfer of service?

The terms and conditions we encountered so far are generally an agreement between two entities that "trust each other". Legally speaking it's an *Intuitu Personae* agreement, as it is not transferable *a priori*.

There's no reference to agreement transfer. During my research, I have not encountered such a case. It appears that neither Microsoft nor Amazon or Google is considering, for the moment, to transfer services that are actually the future of their businesses. However, this is an issue that needs to be considered and discussed with providers whose size or financial health could result in the divestiture of their activities.

On the other hand, the concept of business or services termination is mentioned, as for example in this clause of the AWS client contract:

"THE SERVICE OFFERINGS ARE PROVIDED "AS IS." EXCEPT TO THE EXTENT PROHIBITED BY LAW, OR TO THE EXTENT ANY STATUTORY RIGHTS APPLY THAT CANNOT BE EXCLUDED, LIMITED OR WAIVED, WE AND OUR AFFILIATES AND LICENSORS (A) MAKE NO REPRESENTATIONS OR WARRANTIES OF ANY KIND, WHETHER EXPRESS, IMPLIED, STATUTORY OR OTHERWISE REGARDING THE SERVICE OFFERINGS OR THE THIRD-PARTY CONTENT, AND (B) DISCLAIM ALL WARRANTIES, INCLUDING ANY IMPLIED OR EXPRESS WARRANTIES (I) OF MERCHANTABILITY, SATISFACTORY QUALITY, FITNESS FOR A PARTICULAR PURPOSE, NON-INFRINGEMENT, OR QUIET ENJOYMENT, (II) ARISING OUT OF ANY COURSE OF DEALING OR USAGE OF TRADE, (III) THAT THE SERVICE OFFERINGS OR THIRD-PARTY CONTENT WILL BE UNINTERRUPTED, ERROR FREE OR FREE OF HARMFUL COMPONENTS, AND (IV) THAT ANY CONTENT WILL BE SECURE OR NOT OTHERWISE LOST OR ALTERED."

Amazon indicates that it reserves the right to stop a service without the customer being able to do anything about it. Of course, from a purely professional point of view, it's safe to say that Amazon will not act in a cavalier manner and stop overnight a service that hundreds, thousands or even millions of customers use. Similarly, Microsoft refers to the use of subcontractors and states in clause 11 of the terms of service that it will not subcontract any service without the prior written consent of the client (to comply with EU law).

In any case, cloud service providers generally reserve the right to stop, outsource or transfer their services. But they do it in good business intelligence. It is, therefore, the responsibility of the customer to stay informed and read all the communications from his provider.

Responsibility

You are in your autonomous car with your spouse and your two children. While your vehicle is engaged at a normal pace in a relatively narrow two-way street, a pedestrian starts to cross just a few meters ahead of your car. In a fraction of a second, the artificial intelligence that drives your car is confronted with three choices:

1. Steer to the left to avoid the pedestrian, which would, unfortunately, lead to getting into the truck that comes in front of you;
2. Hit the pedestrian at the risk of killing him or seriously injuring him;
3. Steer to the right to avoid the pedestrian, at the expense of hitting the street light pole that stands on the sidewalk.

It is indeed impossible to stop in time, the space between the pedestrian and the vehicle is too short considering the speed of the latter. What choice to make, knowing that in all cases there may be one or more injured? Once the choice has been made and the accident occurred, who will be held accountable? The owner of the car, its designer, the computer that drives it, the pedestrian who should have looked before crossing or the legislator who authorized the autonomous cars on the streets?

This kind of question is on the agenda of scientists, jurists, and politicians. Until now, decisions were made by human beings, machines like computers were only crutches. It was therefore easy to put someone in the dock and to work to demonstrate guilt or to prove innocence. But when the decision is made by a computer, can one put the latter in the dock and apply a presumption of innocence?

Of course, you're going to tell me that it's going to take a few years to see autonomous cars on our streets. Let us take another example, a real one, which occurred on May 6, 2010. At 2, this May 6, an American broker passed a sales order of several tens of thousands of futures contracts on the S&P 500, one of the indexes of the New York Stock Exchange. Brokerage software and other brokers interpreted this sale as an "insider information", who used information that others have not yet and sold their futures contracts. In just over ten minutes panic spreads to the stock market and the whole stock market collapsed, losing about ten percent, then picking up a few hours later, closing however down by more than three percent.

The US Securities and Exchange Commission would reveal a little later that panic was partly due to a defective algorithm in high-frequency trading computers. Imagine that, on that day, your broker had made you lose a large part of your savings. Who do you hold responsible? The broker, the bank, the software designer, the computer? In the case of the stock exchange, the case is clear since you are generally warned that investing in the stock market carries risks up to the total loss of your capital or even more if you use levers. But, it is not specified in the signed contract that your money is entrusted to a computer that will play with it.

Both examples are symbolic of a legal headache created by the rapid evolution of computer systems, the cloud, and artificial intelligence. This second cannot, for the moment at least, go without the first.

We have seen in the preceding pages that issues of confidentiality, sovereignty or contract are neither anecdotal nor totally properly dealt with today. It has become clear that technology is going much faster than law, even though some states have accelerated the movement, as seen in Europe with the GDPR. However, artificial intelligence and cloud-related technologies are not without adding a layer of complexity requiring reflection on the notion of responsibility.

The legal definition of artificial intelligence

The legal definition of artificial intelligence does not exist! As simple as that. Indeed, it has not been the subject of a proper legislation proper to define its outlines. If we understand what artificial intelligence is in broad terms, there are as many definitions as there are researchers who specialize in these technologies. However, one can agree on the fact that an AI is an electronic, computer or mechanical device for solving a complex problem, requiring a form of intelligence and learning. It is also possible to rely on ISO/IEC 2382:2015: "interdisciplinary field, usually regarded as a branch of computer science, dealing with models and systems for the performance of functions generally associated with human intelligence, such as reasoning and learning". However, in saying this, we haven't really said anything, because an AI like Deep Blue or AlphaGo is very "narrow", since only being programmed to, respectively, play chess or the game of Go. We also realize that most of the AI available today are relatively narrow, because focusing on a single problem, like playing a game, making weather forecasts or driving a car.

We understand that driving a car or flying a plane seems more complex than playing chess, even if only by the risk that the driver or pilot carries for the passengers and his environment, while the chess player cannot, *a priori*, kill anyone by making a mistake. In the case of the chess player, the responsibility for the failure or the success of the game is not seen in the same way as that of the pilot in case of the crash of the airplane. Therefore, if the issues of confidentiality, contract or intellectual property are of particular interest to states, service providers and consumer protection agencies, those of liability in the event of an incident matter to lawyers, insurance companies, and human rights defenders.

Deus Ex Machina

is the machine responsible for its actions, particularly in the event of an incident, accident or unfortunate decision? Divine justice will not come out of the machine to solve the problem. So, what about the notion of responsibility.

Responsibility is a word that is used in many contexts: personal, professional, social, moral, etc. However, the Free Dictionary[40] gives a relatively simple definition based on US law: "The obligation to answer for an act done, and to repair any injury it may have caused." This obligation is directly tied to what law defines as a natural person, either directly in the case of an adult or indirectly in the case of a child or a machine, that an adult has in custody.

The notion of custody, allowing to qualify the responsibility of the fact of the thing, is a legal trick. The responsibility to the individual who is deemed to have the power of use, direction, and control over this thing involved in the damaging action. This, however, presupposes that we have the ability to influence the operation and decisions of IA. If this is undeniable about the many machines we

---

[40] https://legal-dictionary.thefreedictionary.com/responsibility

have control of, this is subject to discussion on machines with some form of intelligence.

Of course, we can question these intelligent abilities and introduce safeguards. In 2015, there were two victims of robots in the automotive industry. One in France and another one in Germany. In both cases, robotic arms seized the victims as if they were metal parts. And in both cases, the investigations found that the victims were not in the security perimeter. However, the question of liability arises. Is the victim responsible for this accident, the employer for failing to put in place an increased security or the designer of the robot for lack of security system allowing to make the distinction between a human being and a metal plate? In this case, however, can we talk about artificial intelligence, even if these arms are highly reconfigurable, connected and in constant improvement?

If we had the ability to question the robotic arm to collect the evidence (this can now make us smile, but it will happen faster than we think, and the consultation of the operating logs can be likened to a form of collection of testimony, as well as watching the film of a surveillance camera), what would this robot tell us? That he regrets his gesture? That he had not realized that it was a human operator and not a metal plate as usual because their weights were similar? Understand Sir, my client is blind, he has no eyes, he sees only through his sensors!

The fact is that an artificial intelligence takes autonomous decisions, without it being possible to determine the human responsibility of its programming because it is designed to transcend this programming and to replace its designer. Considers services like chatbots (see the appendix Chatbots, page 231), which tend to totally replace human operators. Do they respond as a human being? We can doubt it. As the best have now access, in real time, to a set of information about the client that triggers the discussion. A human being instead would not probably access and treat this set of information at that speed. Artificial intelligence and a clear majority of cloud services are designed to increase human capacity, not to replicate them. For Microsoft, IA "increases human ingenuity through intelligent technologies"[41] ». So, we are clearly in an approach that goes beyond the human? But not beyond his responsibilities!

In fact, insofar as artificial intelligence is not human and civil liability applies only to human beings, it is not possible to apply it to AI. As a French lawyer, Stéphane Larrière[42], pointed out, if Siri (IA of Apple) to the question of her civil liability is answering a shocking "no comment", it is that by a flaw of the foundation, it has no legal answer to make: it civil liability is a bug! In other words, the civil liability of an AI or an AI service is not coded!

We are beyond the human! This is not without posing an additional problem: if the AI amplifies the human, and the human follows the recommendations of an AI, is the human being totally responsible to the extent that he cannot fully understand the foundations of this recommendation? Can we now put a level of responsibility that is attributable to human beings and another to AI?

Science without conscience

Let us stop for a moment on this path of the responsibility of artificial intelligence. In fact, we seek to determine the liability in the case of an incident, an accident or a fault. In general, we seek this responsibility to allow compensation, whether moral, legal or pecuniary. But to do this, it is necessary to be aware that there has been an accident, an offense or a crime.

And maybe that's where the problem lies. The law is made to allow society harmoniously by balancing freedoms, obligations, and discipline, between men. Introducing an artificial intelligence disrupts this balance, but the machine is not aware of it. This is what the law seeks to understand the case of mentally disturbed people. A madman may not be responsible for his acts because he is not aware of them. But, until proven otherwise, we are talking about artificial intelligence and not artificial consciousness. Because an AI is not aware of its decisions or actions unless these social, moral or religious rules have been included in its calculation parameters. It would still be necessary to assimilate this to a form of consciousness, which is not yet the case.

---

[41] https://www.microsoft.com/en-us/ai/default.aspx
[42] http://laloidesparties.fr/responsabilite-ia (article in French)

Thus, to quote Stéphane Larrière, "... even if an artificial intelligence interferes in human affairs by acting independently, it cannot, in fact, respond to its actions and the resulting damage." In other words, whatever the degree or nature of its own "fault", it eludes it, as it escapes its own autonomy and initiative, thus disqualifying all responsibility for artificial intelligence. ».

In France, the France AI synthesis report[43] states the following: "the development of artificial intelligence imposes a reflection on automatic decision-making with legal consequences, their transparency and the responsibility attached to these decisions. Many legislative or regulatory provisions (the liability for the facts, the liability of defective products, victims of a traffic accident, etc.) should be reassessed by integrating these new issues". In other words, there is a huge legal blur and no, until now, jurisprudence.

The Commission on Legal Affairs of the European Commission has called for the creation of a legal personality specific to robots, so that at least the most sophisticated autonomous robots can be considered as "electronic persons" with specific rights and duties, including the right to repair any damage caused to a third party. Would be considered as an electronic person any computerized system, that makes autonomous decisions intelligently or interacts independently with third parties. In a draft report dated May 2016[44]. If the Commission mentions the term robot, it specifies in several other places the blurred line between robots and artificial intelligence.

However, the problem is clearly posed: it is necessary to equip the AI with a full legal personality, that of "electronic person".

The AI, itching powder or opportunity for insurance companies

An article from Fortune magazine in January 2017[45] Reported the replacement of 34 employees of a Japanese insurance company with artificial intelligence. If this is only a beginning, this trend appears to be well underway in many industries, from finance to surgery to musical composition, and of course

---

[43] https://www.economie.gouv.fr/files/files/PDF/2017/
Rapport_synthese_France_IA_.pdf
[44] http://www.europarl.europa.eu/sides/getDoc.do?type=COMPARL&reference=PE-582.443&format=PDF&language=FR&secondRef=01
[45] http://fortune.com/2017/01/06/japan-artificial-intelligence-insurance-company/

autonomous vehicles. However, this is only one of many aspects of AI and cloud services that enter the insurance industry: fraud detection, risk prediction, image analysis to allow claims compensation, etc.

If AI will, therefore, help insurers to do their job better and may replace many jobs in the insurance industry, these IA are not without serious problems when it comes to ensuring the facts and actions.

As we have seen so far, AI cannot be assimilated to humans, but they cannot be fully attached to them as would be minors to their parents or employees to their employers. It is this reason that leads to the creation of the legal personality of an electronic person. However, the legal framework will only happen well after the first accidents have taken place. The latter, rare, have already taken place. We met in previous pages the first industrial killer robots. Recently the autopilot of a Tesla killed its first victim, as was revealed by Forbes magazine in July 2016[46].

Although this death is to be deplored, Tesla shared the following figures: this death occurred after 209 million of kilometers traveled with the autopilot on. With human drivers, the United States count one death every 152 million kilometers and worldwide, it's one every 97 million kilometers. We are in a battle of numbers far beyond the perception that we can have about artificial intelligence security. However, it is these figures that allow insurance to pool the risk and, in fact, allow everyone to get insurance at a reasonable cost.

However, in the case of the autonomous car, the insurers remind us that, until now, the driver of the vehicle is fully responsible, as defined by the Vienna Convention on Road Traffic[47]. Moreover, article 8 defines the notion of the driver: " Every moving vehicle or combination of vehicles shall have a driver". If it is an AI that drives, then the AI is the driver of the vehicle. If paragraph 5 defines that "every driver shall at all times be able to control his vehicle", 5 bis introduces the concept of "vehicle system", to which we can assimilate our AI.

---

[46] https://www.forbes.com/sites/briansolomon/2016/06/30/the-first-self-driving-car-death-launches-tesla-investigation
[47] https://www.unece.org/fileadmin/DAM/trans/conventn/Conv_road_traffic_EN.pdf and amendment https://www.unece.org/fileadmin/DAM/trans/doc/2014/wp1/ECE-TRANS-WP1-145e.pdf

This is what this paragraph says: " Vehicle systems which influence the way vehicles are driven shall be deemed to be in conformity with paragraph 5 of this Article and with paragraph 1 of Article 13, when they are in conformity with the conditions of construction, fitting and utilization according to international legal instruments concerning wheeled vehicles, equipment, and parts which can be fitted and/or be used on wheeled vehicles. Vehicle systems which influence the way vehicles are driven and are not in conformity with the aforementioned conditions of construction, fitting and utilization, shall be deemed to be in conformity with paragraph 5 of this Article and with paragraph 1 of Article 13, when such systems can be overridden or switched off by the driver."

In fact, our AI, defined as a vehicle system, needs to be defined in the "international legal instruments" or be able to be neutralized or disabled by the driver. To the extent that it does not conform, since it does not have a legal definition, it must, therefore, be able to be neutralized, which implies a human operator. Case closed!

It is urgent to change the law. However, in anticipation of providing the IA with a legal definition (the electronic person referred to above), it is necessary to quickly introduce what jurists call "no-fault liability". In other words, the manufacturer will be responsible for his autonomous AI, required to prove what caused the accident: a defective object, an algorithmic problem or a mechanical defect. Some manufacturers, like Google, Volvo or Mercedes, have also announced that they will assume the legal responsibility of their autonomous vehicles, and therefore of the AI driving them, in case of accidents.

It will still be necessary for the manufacturers/designers of these IA to agree to share the numerical results of these inquiries. This presupposes the possible access to these data by the investigators, so as not to put these constructors/designers in a position of judge and party.

The other way is to group the responsibilities: Vehicle owner, user, software designer, manufacturer. The victim will be compensated by this group, instructing each of its members to fend for each other, according to the contracts that bind them. But there is still a problem and not the least.

In the case of a fault of human origin, the legislator generally foresees and circumscribes the damages. However, as Stéphane Larrière notes: "For an artificial intelligence, these damages and risks do not exist since the unknown mathematical and behavioral that preside to the indetermination of artificial intelligence propel them in a digital beyond that is not in itself measurable ..., except perhaps by another artificial intelligence..." In other words, how could we poor humans, who are no longer able to apprehend and understand the decisions of an AI, foresee and circumscribe the damage generated by this AI?

In summary, liability in the event of damage caused by an AI will not stop to be much written about, to fuel debates and to provoke discussions between philosophers and jurists. The fact is that, depending on the AI services used in the cloud, it is necessary to approach a lawyer specialized in digital technologies in order to evaluate as completely as possible the risks associated with the unfortunate decisions of IA.

Conclusion

Law is a science, governed by rules, jurisprudence, and laws. The agreement between a client and a service provider cannot cover one hundred percent of the cases, but it must be able to benefit both parties, from professional services.

In the previous pages, we saw that the abandonment of a part of its sovereignty was for the benefit of a quality service at an infinitely lower cost than it would be if we had to manage the entire service itself. It's a subtle balance.

On the other hand, in terms of data protection, security, and confidentiality, cloud services are generally superior to what a customer could afford. We find in most of the countries a legal framework that protects the personal data of both the customers and the providers and limits the access.

Finally, we have seen that the applicable law can quickly become a real headache and that there is a strong bet that the coming years will see countries working more together to define adequate legal frameworks for defending the rights of citizens and enterprises. Until now, if the large countries agree, the smaller ones are left to the good care of the great, in a paternalistic neo-colonialism. However, countries such as South Africa, Mauritius or Rwanda are showing the way. By defining private data protection frameworks, they force providers to review their business models and establish themselves locally to stay on good terms with local businesses and people. The future is in the cloud, but a "glocal" cloud, respectful of local laws adapted to a globalized world.

Legislation

5. Best practices

« The memory is made of practical drawers that open or close to simplify our lives. It's a sign of mediocrity to want to remember everything. »

The tears of Lucifer, René-Jean Clot

The cloud as any technology is easy to implement, provided you start with the right end. It is indeed very easy to fail masterfully. I had the opportunity to meet customers whose deployment of SaaS technologies have proved particularly difficult for many reasons: technological, financial or human.

If you have read the previous pages, you have realized the many facets of the cloud and its impact on your organization. To help you in your cloud project, I propose six essential aspects of the implementation of any cloud project. This collection of good practices is not intended to be exhaustive. Each case is unique and must consider its own realities. It must be the subject of a project on its own.

In fact, we tend to think that the cloud is easy. Some service providers have contributed to this myth. While it is true that the implementation of cloud projects has been facilitated and has accelerated these last years, the pitfalls are numerous and often well hidden. Only an initial assessment and a well-framed project will make the integration of the cloud and the appropriate technologies easy.

The following best practice collection is the result of several years of client projects carried out with success, but not without pain. From the deployment of a few seats in SaaS to the integration of artificial intelligence technologies for several thousand users. This collection revolves around six themes that we have encountered in the previous pages:

- Network
- Costs
- Applications
- Data
- Change
- Specialists

These six themes look at in this order or not, allow us to discover the main pitfalls of a cloud project and to increase its chances of success. One last word before we start detailing those best practices. If I seem alarmist, it is that the cloud carries an incredible hope and that it is terrible to disappoint this hope through sloppy planning and self-satisfied optimism. As with many techniques and technologies, marketing has done its job to make it seem like a wonderful world. The road that allows us to join this wonderful world is not as straightforward as it is thought to be at first glance. Forewarned is forearmed! You are now warned and on the verge of having the proper preparation to make this trip the most enjoyable and effective!

Start with a network assessment

The number one reason for the failure of a cloud project is often found in the arcane of the network. The architecture and the segmentation of the network are arts on their own. For our happiness, and especially that of network technicians and engineers, the generalization of TCP/IP and Ethernet has made the design of networks infinitely easier than at a not-so-far-away era, when one had to manage the coexistence of several technologies, like Token Ring, very popular in the 80's and 90's.

However, and this is where problems often arise, there are subtle differences between a LAN (Local Area Network), WAN (Wide Area Network) and the Internet. Relying on an ADSL or SDSL connection and hoping that your cloud project will work properly is a virtual guarantee of failure. You will still be able to fill the gaps with more bandwidth, but at a generally prohibitive cost. It is, therefore, necessary to think about the topology of your network upstream.

Topology and address plan

The first questions concern the topology of your network. Do you have a plan? If you have multiple sites, how are these connected? What about your current Internet connections?

It is important to understand the data flows on your network to find the bottlenecks. A LAN that works properly is a prerequisite to a WAN that works properly. If the first one is lame, the WAN will not compensate for its deficiencies.

A thorough study of routing and speed between the points of your network will highlight the elements to be improved. For example, a `traceroute` will allow discovering the route that the data packets follow between two points, which a priori seems connected directly. Never forget that physical and logical topologies are two well separated things. Over time and changes in your organization, the evolutions of the physical topology have been able to create a complex situation at the logical level and cause incessant traffic jams on certain parts of the network.

The first step in cloud good practice is to ensure that your local network is working properly. That fast access without error to all its resources is possible. This seems to be obvious, yet many organizations still work with 10-base T networks and serial-bound hubs. This is not particularly shocking, but when the cloud performance issues are going to pop up, we will have to start from scratch and it all starts with the local network. As mentioned previously, the cloud is not the solution to all evils and especially not to the local network bad performance. So always start with the latter to optimize the speed.

Once the LAN is sorted out, the WAN can be addressed, especially in remote areas. Star topologies are often seen on the African continent, in which remote offices are connected to headquarters in dial-up or VSAT. The WAN connection then becomes the bottleneck. This point and these connections are to be dealt apart. I come back to bandwidth in the next section.

To-do!

Three essential steps:

1. Establish a plan of your network, both physical and logical, indicating the speed of all connections. This will allow you to identify potential bottlenecks.
2. Clean your address plan, both internally and externally. This will probably allow you to reorganize your IP addresses and to bring clarity to your different network segments.
3. Implement all the necessary changes to simplify topology and address plan.

This seems to be common sense but know that any deviation will have a cost in terms of bandwidth requirement. An immediate correction saves many subsequent costs.

Authentication and replication

Users of a network authenticate to a directory server. For security reasons and key validity, this server is frequently queried. A recommendation is often then to distribute servers across all remote offices to have local authentication. Authentication is only part of a gigantic data and application security iceberg. Here are some authentication-related activities that will have an impact on network operations:

- User authentication to the enterprise directory
- User authentication to applications when they do not rely on the enterprise directory
- User authentication to applications when they rely on the enterprise directory
- Distributing and validating encryption keys
- Distributing and validating group policies (GPO)

- Single-Sign-On (SSO) when multiple directories are synchronized to support only one user authentication to access multiple systems and applications
- Multi-factor authentication, by using a smart card, mobile application, SMS or another mechanism
- Call to the Rights Management Service when accessing protected documents

This list is not exhaustive but gives you a glimpse of what can happen in the background when you perform benign operations on the network, such as launching an application, accessing a document or printing this document (there may be permissions to access printers that will require directory lookup).

This authentication, identity check, and access traffic can be high, and even, very high. If it stays on a local network, there is a good chance that it will be painless for the user, but the more you are going to strengthen the security, the more likely this traffic will increase. To the point, that some user-induced operations can generate traffic specific to this authentication which will then considerably slow down the user's machine that can go so far as to cause it to freeze or feel like freeze since network operations are slow.

By adding a cloud layer, these operations can then degrade the user experience that will lose valuable time to wait. It is important to put yourself on the side of the user to assess the experience. It is the latter that will make your project a success or not. But the authentication traffic is not the only one involved.

A personal anecdote illustrates the other part of the directories. A few years ago, during a professional stay abroad, the hotel that hosted me offered the internet to its residents, limiting its use to 1 GB per day. At first glance, this seemed ample enough to carry out my work outside of my hours at the local office. However, great was my surprise when after a small hour I had already exhausted my quota. 1 GB in an hour? While I had only read and replied to a few emails and work on a presentation for a customer the next day! I was intrigued, and I wanted to know the culprit. Was it the ten-minute communication that I had on voice over IP with Skype for Business? Was it the mail download? After a few minutes of research, these operations were eliminated, consuming only a few megabytes. In fact, the culprit suddenly appeared: the automatic replication of my files with OneDrive. No security issues here, but replication. How does this relate to directory issues? Well, the latter must also be replicated to be synchronized!

Whether you are using an OpenLDAP directory, Red Hat Directory Service, Microsoft Active Directory, or other, this directory replication occurs at constant intervals. If one remains on a local network, the speed of the latter is generally not or little impacted by the replication of the directory. However, as soon as the network opens to the cloud and a directory needs to be synchronized, you need to stop for a moment and plan this replication properly.

All cloud providers offer directory services in the cloud: from Amazon Cloud directory to Azure Active directory or from Oracle Internet directory to Google G Suite domain. If all go out of their way to ease the life of the network administrator and ultimately that of the user, it is not without sometimes obscuring the technical realities of replication and especially its impact on the network. If you have a dozen users, the question of the impact of replication does not arise and will probably not arise. However, several hundred or even thousands of users and objects (computers, printers, phones, etc.) on your network may make your connection totally unusable!

To-Do!

If you have your topology and address plan, as previously stated, add authentication streams, domain controllers, LDAP servers, and any machine that can provide authentication to your network plan. Then ask your network manager the following two things:

1. All authentication and security services and their location on the network

2. The directory replication streams.

Then, rationalize those streams, restricting replication, and concentrating services on the LAN.

Internet connection and bandwidth

The question everyone asks: How much bandwidth do I need? There is no automatic answer and no magic wand, but some thinking is required. A first step is necessary: Internet or not?

In fact, mixing up cloud and the internet is almost a sin. Your cloud services are an extension of your data center, so they are an integral part of your extended network. Thus, relying on a public Internet connection, even secure, is probably not the best option.

Figure 5-1 -Internet connection and cloud

Considering that the cloud services you subscribe to are an extension of your own data center, a point-to-point connection between your data center and your cloud provider or an IPVPN connection between your WAN and the data center of your provider may make perfect sense. It's therefore very important to differentiate between an Internet connection and cloud connection. The first one allows users to use Internet services, access private or public websites. The second allows them to access the cloud services that your organization subscribes to, such as messaging, file backup, or database services, to take just a few examples.

There are several technical ways to connect to a remote data center and you will need to discuss this with your Internet service provider or telecommunications provider to decide on the best possible and affordable connection. Going in the technical details of such connections is beyond the scope of this book, however, take the following elements into consideration when choosing the connection type:

137

1. *What bandwidth do you need to connect to cloud services?* This issue is not obvious, as the needs vary depending on the number of users and their consumption of these services. A very basic rule that works in most of the cases is to consider that a user who consumes messaging, file and voice over IP services will require between 1 Mbps and up to 100 Mbps if he is a large consumer of videos (Video-conference, training with online video, etc.). About 100 users will between 100 Mbps and 10Gbps, and presumably, a choice between 500Mbps and 1Gbps seems reasonable. Most of the access providers will allow you to start at the bottom of the range, to let you carry out the necessary tests and then to increase if need be.

2. *Are the circuits redundant?* In general, access providers will offer you redundant logic circuits on the same physical circuit. If you do not have full confidence in the physical circuit, it is usually possible to establish a redundant connection through two or more different physical circuits. For example, a Kenyan customer may want to have a main connection through fiber going North and a secondary connection through fiber going South. This will make it possible to cope with an emergency situation in the event that a fiber has been physically cut, as has happened in the past.

3. *Are your routers, switches, and hubs redundant?* What is the point in setting up redundancy in communications with the data center if your weakest link Is the connection to your network? Setting up redundancy at the edge of your network is generally economical and simple. Why do without it?

4. *What about security?* It's a topic that deserves a whole book! However, once the connection solution is chosen, it is appropriate to correctly position the security elements of the network. If the cloud provider guarantees the protection of its infrastructures, you will need to protect your services, applications, and access: firewall, prevention of denial of services (DoS), prevention and detection of intrusions (IDS/IPS), virtual private network, traffic isolation, access policies, access control (ACL), routing, to name a few. It is also generally possible to implement some of these elements (such as firewalls, IDS/IPS), as virtual machines hosted by the cloud provider. It is therefore highly recommended to

proceed with a safety plan of your installations once the type of connection is chosen.

The conclusion of this part should be clear: keep Internet and cloud apart, dedicate a connection to cloud services, size and secure it to provide the best possible level of performance and security for your users.

To Do!

1. Explore possible connections between your organization and the data center, focusing on VLAN connections.

2. Evaluate your needs in terms of bandwidth and measure it constantly.

3. Find and eliminate individual points of failure, to have a redundant connection chain.

4. Enhance security at all connection points.

Now that you've covered the network, let's look at the applications you're going to access. The purpose of a cloud connection is to consume services, either new or the ones you will migrate to the cloud.

Applications, communications, and executions

While most modern applications are designed for the cloud and to operate on virtual machines, it is not the same for older applications that have not been thought with the cloud in mind. Even a virtual machine, hosting applications in your data center may not work the same when moved to a cloud datacenter.

If you consider the routing, the address translation, the security layers, the latency and all the elements added between the client and the application, the latter may not react as expected. In fact, there is little chance that it runs in the same way at first glance. So here we are back in the world of hybrid data centers.

Figure 5-2 - Hybrid Cloud Architecture

Unless you are what we call a "pure player", that is, an organization born in the cloud, there is a strong bet that you have existing applications and infrastructure. If your entire infrastructure is already virtualized, you will avoid some cold sweats. If not, the first step is to test applications running on physical servers in a virtual environment. All those who do not pass this test will be kept locally or updated if such an evolution is possible. The others will be put on virtual servers.

The next question is the physical platform. Most cloud providers support Intel's x86 architectures, but, for example, rarely Oracle's SPARC architectures.

Shifting an application on a virtual machine in the cloud is not always a healthy walk because of its dependencies. It can depend on other applications, databases or various services of the operating system, the network, or even the virtual machine itself. If these dependencies are many, complex, or even unknown, the application will simply not work.

Not all applications are born equal!

Some applications will simply not run on a virtual machine in the cloud. The reasons can be multiple, and it would be tedious to list them here. This is one of the reasons why the immediate future of the cloud is hybrid. In about ten years or perhaps more, it will be possible for all organizations to free themselves completely from their data centers. Some have already made that choice. The result will be felt on the ability of these organizations to innovate, reinvent themselves and focus on their core business.

Waiting to be able to update all the applications needed for an organization, the hybrid cloud is an inevitable step. This is equivalent to classifying applications into three categories:

1. Those that cannot be virtualized, and must either be dropped or updated to virtualized versions;

2. Those that are virtualized in the local data center;

3. The ones that are brought into the cloud.

Each of these categories will have a different evolutionary schedule that can lead to a total cloud setting or a strategic conservation of the hybrid model. The goal remains the optimum use of each of the organization's resources according to the constraints imposed on them.

It is then once more crucial to precisely mapping all applications and their functional, logical and physical dependencies. This unavoidable exercise is the prerequisite for shifting the application. At the end of this exercise, it will be possible to carry out the shifting and execution tests from the cloud.

One of the stumbling blocks of the application cloud shifting remains the communication of these applications with the customer and the other dependent components. If, for example, over the years, the client-server model gave way to the decoupled model of the Internet, there are still a plethora of applications developed in client-server mode and strongly dependent on relational databases.

Others depend on files or documents stored locally on the user's machine. For the past ten years, with the introduction of HD video and high-resolution images, the size of these files has continued to increase. To the point that it is common to see PowerPoint presentations, Word documents or Excel spreadsheets reach sizes of more than 100 MB. Moving such files is consuming a massive amount of bandwidth. An application running in the cloud to access a file stored locally on the user's machine will not only run slowly but also put the network on its knees. The same goes for an application running locally that has access to large documents stored on the network.

One aspect of the cloud lift and shift is therefore not only the architecture of the applications but their execution and communication. These elements may limit the evolution of certain applications to the cloud.

To Do!

No cloud without applications to run. However, not all applications are born equal in the cloud, it is necessary to know the ones that can be lifted and those that will not support it.

1. Catalog all applications and their modes of communications.

2. Test them all in cloud mode to study operation and usability.

3. Set up a roadmap for converting applications to the cloud and go for it!

Finally, it may be the same with the use of local resources such as printers or scanners. What worked with acceptable local performance can see its functioning degrade once in the cloud. The cloud is not always the magic wand that certain would like it to be.

In the previous discussion, we introduced the question of storage. For many customers, it's central. Confidentiality, security, and sovereignty are written in flashing letters before any other consideration. However, if logically, the provider contractually guarantees these three important characteristics of information storage, it is necessary to consider the classification of the data. That is the purpose of the next part.

Encryption on all levels

No cloud without encryption. All is said in these four words. So of course, if all your data is public, you can ask yourself the question of the validity of this assertion. Even the most harmless information must be protected so that it is not untimely modified. This applies naturally to the encryption.

"Data is the new oil"! Oil requires being handled with caution, as it can ignite and explode. The same goes for the data. Especially since all, even confidential ones can be shared.

An example of a digital puzzle

Medical information stored in the patient management system of a hospital is highly confidential and its access is restricted. It's therefore essential that they are encrypted. The Ministry of Health, to define public health policies, has to recover statistics on diseases and their treatments. These statistics can only be established by having access to the confidential data of the hospitals, which are encrypted. This can quickly become the nightmare of the network administrator, who should not have access to the patient data. So how do you share encrypted data that need to be anonymized? Knowing that all this can be done automatically with artificial intelligence and business intelligence systems, without any human intervention. Sharing while protecting!

Encryption and cryptographic keys

To encrypt data, you need a cryptographic key. Anyone with this key can decrypt the data. This is the basis of any encryption system, the modern Enigma machine. The question of storage, audit, and protection of this key arises naturally. A bit like the bank vault, the Key management system is central. It is usually accompanied by a level of physical security, such as smart cards or biometrics. In any case, it is to be defined at the beginning of the encryption policy.

What to encrypt?

Everything! Data stored in databases (most database management systems provide encryption at the level of each table column), unstructured data such as Hadoop data, files, and folders on the servers, personal computers, and mobile devices. And this at all levels: encryption of the hard disks of the virtual machines and storage bays attached thereto, encryption of the disks of the network storage bays, Layer-2 encryption of all communications between servers and services, encryption of the disks of the personal computers, tablets and smartphones. You see where I'm going to. When I told you everything, that's everything! This helps to protect the entire organization's information in depth.

You're going to tell me that this is all a bit of paranoia. Absolutely not! A cryptographic system is only valid if it is complete. Imagine that you do not encrypt the contents of the employees' smartphones. So what, would you ask? Knowing that about a quarter of these materials is lost or stolen, it is not impossible for one of your collaborators' smartphones to fall into the hands of ill-intentioned people. If they cannot enter the phone system that will be protected by a password, they will be able to disassemble the device to reach the storage memory and extract its content. Without encryption, no protection and it is the whole organization that has just been compromised. The number of scandals due to data leaks is there to remind us that data protection, starting with their encryption, is not a vain word.

To Do!

Encryption is not a « *nice to have* », it's a must.

1. Encrypt the storage of all devices connected to your network: servers, personal computers, tablets, and telephones.

2. Encrypt all communications between these devices.

3. Store encryption keys safely.

Go back to work: Evaluate your internal encryption, that of your cloud provider and decide what to activate or add if there are loopholes. Again, work with the security department of your organization (if you don't have one, you'll have to think about it seriously) to guarantee the encryption of all information across the organization!

Classification of data

We've all heard about Confidential or Top-Secret data. If for most people, these two terms mean the same thing, they define different classes of information. Let us pause for a moment on this notion of data classification through simple examples.

My address is known to the mailman (yes, they still exist) and potentially to everyone. It can be considered to be public information. My phone number can be private. I can give it to my friends, but not make it public so as not to be disturbed time and time again. The balance of my savings account is an information that my banker and I have only access to. If the information is not completely confidential, its access is limited to a small number of individuals. The fact that I have a chronic illness that compels me to go to the hospital once a week is an information that I may not want to share, even with my best friends, and that will only be kept in my medical record. It is a confidential information that has limited access. The positioning of the nuclear submarines of a country at a given time is an ultra-confidential information concerning the defense of a country. Finally, the trigger codes of the nuclear weapons are top secret and known to an excessively small number of individuals, generally not even knowing the whole of them.

The previous examples give you an idea of the data classification: some are public and have little or no impact on the concerned individuals, others are top secret because of their criticality. It appears that storage and access to the different data classes must be managed in separate ways, with defined rules. The question of their storage or not in the cloud can be then taken logically.

The classification of the data consists of attaching labels that allow defining their value and importance, and thus the protection to be granted. This can also set the location of the data storage. In fact, you may be reluctant to store confidential data in the cloud. However, the question of access, protection, and auditing of these confidential data is still to be asked, which sometimes are not really, technically, confidential, due to their weak protection, their non-existent encryption, and their scope. All this to say that the classification of the data must answer a number of questions in a clear, precise and concise manner.

Authentication and Access Authorization

Before classifying the data, it is necessary to set up an authentication and data access policy. This sounds trivial, but let's start by defining these terms:

- **Authentication**: The Oxford dictionary defines it this way: "The process or action of verifying the identity of a user or process ". Everything is therefore in the identity of the user and the verification that he or she is who he or she claims to be. The easiest mechanism is the famous username-password pair. However, these elements are increasingly stolen and are no longer a guarantee of user authentication. It is, therefore, necessary to put in place complementary means such as biometric elements (fingerprint, facial recognition, etc.), physical elements (smart card, electronic token, etc.) or applications (verification application, SMS, etc.). This multi-factor authentication (MFA) makes it possible to guarantee the identity of the user with a greater certainty and to prevent the theft of a password from being transformed into identity theft. There are many different multi-factor authentication solutions on the market, it's up to you to choose.

145

- **Access control**: Once the user is authenticated, it is necessary to be able to define what it has, or not, access to. Whether it is documents in the form of files, in the form of structured data (e.g. relational database) or not (data lake for example), or applications that manipulate its data. This access control and associated access must be able to be audited in order to detect potential flaws but must be monitored at all times by using behavioral monitoring programs to detect any dubious access attempts or elevation of privilege.

Now that the basics of authentication and access authorization are set, we can look at classifying the data to guarantee its use.

> **Note** As shown above, a prerequisite to the classification of the data is their encryption, during their move, storage or manipulation. Without encryption, the classification loses a crucial ally in the protection of the data.

Terminologies

While states and in particular the military has since immemorial time classify their data for obvious issues of defending their territories, it is not the same as other public or private organizations. Some models are interesting from an intellectual point of view, such as the one described in FIPS 199[48], the standard for classifying U.S. federal information, but complex to implement and not necessarily adapted to the cloud. A good and simple practice is to ask the question of the classification in terms of risks for the company: Low, Moderate, High, and therefore of potential damage in case of disclosure of this information.

As in the previous examples, information disseminated legally in the public is at low, or even null, risk. A document concerning the process of manufacturing a product of the company may have a moderate risk, while the documents describing in detail the future revolutionary product can have a high risk for the future of the company.

---

[48] FIPS 199, Standards for Security Categorization of Federal Information and Information Systems, http://csrc.nist.gov/publications/fips/fips199/FIPS-PUB-199-final.pdf

It is, therefore, necessary to define the vocabulary defining the class in which the document is located according to the risk it potentially poses to the organization.

Risk	Terminologies 1	Terminology 2	Terminology 3
Low	Public	Unlimited	Unprotected
Moderate	Restricted	Limited Internally	Internal
High	Confidential	Secret	Restricted

Table 5-1 - Examples of classification terminology

There are classification systems with four or five levels. However, the complexity of a classification system is inversely proportional to its use. It is infinitely better to have a simple and useful system than a very strong and unused one. The advantage of the classification of risk in three levels: low, moderate and high, is that it is understood by all the employees of the organization. Here is the definition of FIPS 199

- Low: The loss of confidentiality, integrity, or availability could be expected to have a **limited** adverse effect on organizational operations, organizational assets, or individuals.
- Moderate: The loss of confidentiality, integrity, or availability could be expected to have a **serious** adverse effect on organizational operations, organizational assets, or individuals.
- High: The loss of confidentiality, integrity, or availability could be expected to have a **severe or catastrophic** adverse effect on organizational operations, organizational assets, or individuals.

The FIPS 199 then defines the limited, serious and catastrophic effects:

- **Limited**: A limited adverse effect means that, for example, the loss of confidentiality, integrity, or availability might: (i) cause a degradation in mission capability to an extent and duration that the organization is able to perform its primary functions, but the effectiveness of the functions is noticeably reduced; (ii) result in minor damage to organizational assets; (iii) result in minor financial loss; or (iv) result in minor harm to individuals (this last point makes sense in a military context, rarely in a business one).

147

- **Serious**: A serious adverse effect means that, for example, the loss of confidentiality, integrity, or availability might: (i) cause a significant degradation in mission capability to an extent and duration that the organization is able to perform its primary functions, but the effectiveness of the functions is significantly reduced; (ii) result in significant damage to organizational assets; (iii) result in significant financial loss; or (iv) result in significant harm to individuals that does not involve loss of life or serious life threatening injuries
- **Catastrophic**: A severe or catastrophic adverse effect means that, for example, the loss of confidentiality, integrity, or availability might: (i) cause a severe degradation in or loss of mission capability to an extent and duration that the organization is not able to perform one or more of its primary functions; (ii) result in major damage to organizational assets; (iii) result in major financial loss; or (iv) result in severe or catastrophic harm to individuals involving loss of life or serious life threatening injuries.

Although the definitions may evolve from one organization to another, the limits are well defined and can be explained to the employees.

> **Note** We can also define a zero risk for freely available information, such as those published on a website accessible to everyone or spam messages received, which have no value. This risk is associated with the documents, data, and applications of the companies that are not then classified. This greatly facilitates the classification process. It can indeed be assumed that any information that has no impact on the operations or assets of the organization does not need to be classified.

Systems

Once the data classification terminology has been defined, it needs to be implemented. It is, therefore, necessary to have a tool or a set of computer tools that can be used to label information, and to secure and audit access. It is necessary to consider the movement of that information. Thus, secure information sitting on a server or local area network must continue to be secured if it is moved and stored in the cloud, as well as on a mobile device such as a tablet or smartphone.

Figure 5-3 – Information protection systems

To implement the data classification policy, the following systems should be set up, as illustrated in Figure 5-3:

- A directory with access control. Each user must be authenticated and his or her access to the information clearly defined. On the other hand, each access to restricted or confidential data must be logged in a ledger that cannot be altered.
- An encryption process. All data must be encrypted at rest, on the move and during use. This encryption can be done by different systems, at different levels, as we have seen in the previous section, Encryption on all .
- A Rights Management system. This mechanism allows attaching to each information its classification and the persons authorized to access it. This label follows the document wherever it is.
- A Data Loss Prevention system. This is, for example, the base of the PCI DSS (*Payment Card Industry Data Security Standard*), which defines confidential information relating to companies dealing with credit card payments. Such a system protects the exchange and use of data such as credit card or social security number, financial or health data, etc. It is generally based on self-learning mechanisms and complex directories, which enable the automatic detection of information to be protected.

> **To Do!**
>
> All organizations should have a data classification system. In general, it is often implicit. Making it explicit helps to increase document security while protecting them as the organization grows.
>
> 1. Define classification terminology and spread it.
>
> 2. Put in place the rules and the tools to its application.
>
> 3. Audit regularly to ensure proper operation.

We almost reached the end of those best practices to consider before embarking on a cloud computing project. So far, we have studied the main technical aspects of the cloud. However, the best technology is nothing without its adoption by users. It is this aspect that will now interest us.

Driving change

There are only three things that are certain in life: tax, death, and change. For the first two, this book will not bring you any answers. Concerning the third, let's look at it in the context of the cloud.

There are many books and methodologies on change management. This topic is driven by the fact that any change is difficult and yet inevitable. What interests us here is the perceived change by the user, not the change on the IT side. Certainly, the cloud will introduce many disruptions in the management of computer systems. ITIL (Information Technology Infrastructure Library), a set of best practices in the management of IT services, defines change management and the cloud is not different from any other changes. It will generate the needs for new skills, new procedures, and new processes. Basically, the cloud will generate new questions, as we have seen over the previous pages. It will, therefore, be necessary to integrate this into the change management of IT.

On the user side, it is possible that the cloud is painless and odorless. But it's unlikely. The cloud, as we have seen so far, introduces new uses: mobility, security, confidentiality, compliance, etc. As a result, it generates or must generate, new reflexes, new practices and the use of new tools. This will change the daily lives of the users.

An aspect found in almost all cloud projects: the technology and its appropriation by the users are always faster in the personal than the professional field. For example, you get a new smartphone for your birthday. You will connect it to the Internet, download applications and exchange information quickly and without asking too many questions. You will probably develop new habits. And then quickly, you're going to want to connect this device to your corporate network. And, depending on the rules in place, you will, or not, be able to continue to use your phone as before. The questions of encryption, identification, confidentiality, data leakage, information sharing, etc. need to be answered and will certainly have to make you quickly change the habits that you had developed to adopt the one that your company will impose on you. Change can then be experienced as a constraint and potentially lead to circumvention of the rules. We see this every day!

How then to make a change as painless as possible, and adopted? Without going into the details of the many existing methodologies of change management, which is not the topic of this book, it is important to understand and implement the stages of change management. I use here the ADKAR method of Prosci, as I was able to see it at work on Cloud projects carried out by Microsoft Consulting Services.

In its 2016 study on best practices in change management, Prosci demonstrated that:

- 94% of projects accompanied by a change management approach were successful against 15% otherwise, a factor of 6!
- The first contributor to the success of a project was the sponsorship of the management team, just before the structured approach to change.
- 90% of change management practitioners believe that integrating the culture of the company is crucial to the success of any project.

For having lived many successful and failed projects, change management is not an infinitely complex science, but to ignore it is the number one reason for failure. Between 94% and 15%, the choice does not even exist. Change management will slow the implementation of the necessary changes and will have a cost but compared to the financial and organizational cost of a failure, the winner is obvious! So, what needs to be done? Three main steps:

1. Preparing Change
2. Managing Change
3. Reinforcing change

Let's look at his three steps a little more in detail.

Preparing Change

The first questions relate to the nature, size, and impact of the change:

- What are we changing?
- Who will it impact?
- Who is the sponsor of the change?
- Who should be a part of the change management team?
- How long will it take to set up the change in the organization?
- What is the best strategy to implement for the project to be a success?

These questions and their answers will help to highlight the who and what of the change. The third question will mainly make sure that the change goes outside of the IT department to fall into the hands of the sponsor. Without a sponsor and no clear appropriation by this sponsor of the changes to come, the first hurdles, and there will be, will kill the project. The sponsor defines the vision, helps you articulate and disseminate the benefits of the upcoming change, will be your spokesperson in case of difficulties and will be happy to cut the ribbon at the end.

The second phase can begin.

Manage Change

This is the phase that will create the plan and put it into music. The PROSCI methodology proposes five plans:

1. **The Communication plan**. Informing, listening, ensuring that the impacted employees are aware of future changes, understand the benefits and what is expected of them is essential. How to communicate is critical: it is not a question of sending an email to the whole organization to believe that "communication has been done". Which media to use, the correspondents used to relay the message and make sure it's landing. This concept of correspondents is essential. Who

do the employees trust, who do they listen to? These are the people who must become the champions of change.

2. **The sponsorship roadmap**. What do you expect from the sponsor or sponsors? What roles do they play? A specific plan of action should be put in their hands. What messages will they communicate? When? In what forms? I always tend to say that to improvise well, it is necessary first and foremost to repeat. The rehearsal makes the natural. Nothing should be improvised. The sponsor (or sponsors) will probably have no time to devote to creating their messages, so you have to spoon-feed them so that they are at the peak of their performance at the service of the project.

3. **The Training Plan**. Whether the training is online, in the classroom, in the form of mentoring, or self-learning is irrelevant. The important thing is to consider the need for user training. You have to teach them what will change, what is expected of them. Training is a time that must be exciting, so you must consider the construction of this excitement in the training plan. Any new technique or technology can be scary at first glance, challenge the acquired knowledge and disrupt the working methods. It is, therefore, necessary to reinforce the benefits of the project for the organization and its employees and to develop the desire for its implementation among the collaborators.

4. **The Coaching Plan**. The managers of the involved employees must be the vectors of change. They must help their employees to master the new tools, processes, and procedures, after having mastered them first. It is essential that the management is convinced of the benefits of the project and be a change actor.

5. **The Resistance Management Plan**. It is well known that we need to anticipate the problems better before they occur rather than solve them after the facts. The purpose of the resistance management plan is to provide elimination strategies, or in any case decrease, of resistance to change. Which populations will be resisting? How can we help them overcome the obstacles? What activities should be taken to have the change be accepted?

> This reminds me of a project of providing mailboxes in the cloud to thirty thousand employees of an administration. Everyone, starting with the sponsor, was excited. After a difficult effort to list the names of the concerned employees, which was necessary to create the mailboxes, and to the creation of these, after a few months, the rate of utilization was still very low. It was then that the company in charge of the change management realized that only ten percent of the concerned population had access to a device to consult their mailboxes. The resistance to change was not the ones that had been perceived!

Setting up these plans is only the first step, executing the change is key. Then comes the time of execution. However, if everything happens as planned, there is still a third phase, often forgotten: continuity in the time of change.

Reinforcing change

Every project manager knows, nothing ever happens as planned. Problems appear where no one had foreseen, Murphy's law always strikes at the most unexpected moment. It is, therefore, necessary to anticipate and foresee the famous « Plan B ». For that, four key points:

1. **Measure**. To know if the change is effective and the project a success, it is appropriate to measure its impact. In a cloud project, this may be the rate of use of the new application, the increase in the consumption of services, the reduction in the number of calls to support. It is important to anticipate the measures of success. This will make it possible to put in place the corrective measures necessary for the adoption of the new tools, processes, and procedures.
2. **Correct**. What are the causes of the low adoption? What's the catch? What should be changed? Paying attention to the employees is critical at this stage, in order to be able to quickly correct the situation and return to the anticipated measures.
3. **Reinforce**. The human being is a creature of habit. Strengthening the planned behavior is therefore central to the ongoing training process. If not, old habits will take over, or even the new one will be abandoned to the benefit of unexpected others.
4. **Celebrate**. Change is hard, so it is worth celebrating and congratulating the individuals and teams who have crossed the successive stages with

gusto. This also has the effect of reinforcing the message of the need for change.

To Do!

Change is natural, but generally painful. It is essential to accompany it to dramatically increase the chances of success of the Cloud project.

1. Prepare the change by understanding the stakes and risks and having a clear vision of the impacts on the functioning of the organization and its employees.

2. Manage change by communicating, training and coaching, and above all by ensuring that the general management acts as sponsors.

3. Reinforce the change by measuring and correcting the gaps in the expected ideal situation.

Anticipating the difficulties of change and accompanying these changes in working methods are essential to the success of any project impacting individuals and the organization. The cloud is not absent from these upheavals. Unfortunately, management often has the impression that this is an evolution of the back office with little impact on users, if not better or easier. From the moment when we will ask the user to do something new, change there is, and it should be accompanied.

We have one last thing to discuss that is the evolution of jobs. The first reflex is to believe that the cloud will remove jobs, especially on the computer operations. If this can be partly true as we have seen in Chapter 2, Limitations and constraints of the cloud, the cloud will also create jobs, as we will now see.

Cloud Specialist and Data scientist

The Harvard Business Review published a few years ago an article entitled "Data Scientist: The Sexiest Job of the 21st Century"[49]. But who is this individual and

---

[49] https://hbr.org/2012/10/data-scientist-the-sexiest-job-of-the-21st-century

what are her qualities? We will see that this is one of the new jobs that the cloud gave birth to. However, let's start with the cloud basics with the cloud specialist.

The skills and missions of the Cloud Specialist

If you are still with me after these pages, you now have in mind that the cloud is not as simple as just moving virtual machines into a data center, miles away from you. The cloud, therefore, requires special skills, not always simple to find on the market.

The Cloud Specialist is an individual I describe as "protean". He must have more than one string to his bow and above all, a curiosity that make him acquire new skills constantly. Here is, however, a starting base to assess the skills of the cloud specialist:

- **Network**. She must have a good knowledge of IP networks both in LAN and in WAN. As we have seen, the connection between the sites and to the remote data center is critical to the success of a cloud project. No good network, no good cloud!
- **Operating systems**. Linux and Windows must have no secrets. This is a minimum since X86 architectures are prevalent. Some knowledge of the SPARC and Solaris architectures are not to be neglected.
- **Virtualization**. Whether it's Xen, VMware ESX, Hyper-V or Oracle VM Server, virtualization is the cornerstone of any cloud architecture. And the hypervisor, its essential component.
- **Management and operations**. From Network management to DCIM (*Data Center Infrastructure Management*), operational dashboards for patch management, no information should be kept secret to manage and automate the operations of the local data center and its connections to the cloud.
- **Identity and security**. The topic of cybersecurity is a must. LDAP or Active Directory, multifactor authentication, e-mail filtering, access security, Security Information and Event Management (SIEM), encryption, Kerberos, etc. are topics that the cloud specialist should master with the help of the Chief Information Security Officer (CISO).
- **Storage and Database**. If it is the realm of data scientist, the cloud specialist must have good knowledge in document storage with NFS,

HDFS, NTFS to cite only three very common filesystems, and in the database with Hadoop, MySQL, SQL Server, Oracle DB.

- **Development tools**. Again, this is not necessarily its strength, but the basics of PHP, Python, Perl, Ruby, or SQL are appreciated to understand the issues of cloud applications.

If, as you can see, the technical expertise of the cloud specialist is extensive, these are geared toward cloud computing whether local, public and hybrid. It is this last architecture that is most likely to prevail in a majority of organizations. Understanding the technical issues of the implementation of hybrid technologies is paramount.

Her missions will all be at the heart of the information system and the use of local and remote data centers, implementing the characteristics of the cloud. Among her main missions one can cite:

- Choose the cloud provider offering the best solution, responding to the constraints posed by the organization.
- Optimize the data flow between the organization and the data center.
- Propose and validate the technological choices of infrastructures, platforms, and applications in cloud mode.

The cloud specialist will, therefore, be at the forefront of the architecture technological decisions. He must be able to set up the business cases to demonstrate the merits of the cloud choice to the general management and to estimate its return on investment. It will ultimately be on the slate to become the CIO of the organization.

The skills and missions of the Data Scientist

The sexiest job of the twenty-first century! The cloud has promoted and will continue to promote the collection of data. Whether you like it or not, "Big Brother is watching you!", to take up the famous sentence of Georges Orwell's novel, 1984. Smartphones, applications, and connected objects collect data. But a data set is silent. To extract its substantial core, it is necessary to analyze and find the information contained therein. That's the role of Data Scientist.

A job created by cloud computing, it builds on the analyst skillset, with a strong technical orientation. Its basic skills are as follows:

- **Programming**. He's a C++ and Java ace. He knows algorithmic and can code. This forms the basis of the intelligence that he will put in place to "mine the data", that is, extract the information and the trends hidden therein.
- **Relational Database**. She's a champion of the SQL language and the structures of relational databases, such as those stored in SQL Server, Oracle DB or MySQL.
- **Data warehouse**. Über fan of hypercube, measurements, and dimensions, he can aggregate relational data into hypercubes to make dashboards or prepare them to be joined to non-relational data. He must have solid notions of ETL (Extract, Transform, Load).
- **Unstructured data**. Hadoop, data Lake and Big data. How to use vast volumes of unstructured data to carry sentiment analysis or create heuristics.
- **Statistics and mathematics**. Banks have understood this: to put in place their predictive market-room models, they need big, well-rounded minds. The Data scientist must be very comfortable in mathematics and especially in statistical calculations. Without this basic skill, it is very easy to implement totally erroneous models.

As you can see, the data scientist is a versatile and very technical profile. It is no coincidence that the major engineering schools have made it a full-fledged specialty, like the joint Master of Science between ESSEC and CentraleSupélec[50]. Her missions are multiple and varied, usually directly measurable because in connection with sales, production and general management. These include:

- Identification of data sources and choice of data relevant to a desired type of analysis.
- Construction of data warehouses and implementation of ETL procedures.
- Development of prediction models, algorithms for analyzing data and anticipating behaviors.
- Development of dashboards for the managers and the general management.

---

[50] http://www.centralesupelec.fr/en/msc-data-sciences-business-analytics-essec-centralesupelec

- Integration with the production, commercial or marketing systems of data analysis results in real-time.
- Participation in artificial intelligence algorithms.

One of the important points of the job of the data scientist is to make it measurable. The impact of the data scientist must be felt on the results of the organization, either by improving production tools, to produce more and/or better, or by improving sales, by cross-selling or incremental sales, or by improving every critical process.

The miracle of data analysis is that the results are sometimes unexpected. It is a good thing to keep a very open mind while validating the assumptions by verifying that no errors have crept in.

One last point: Big data has evolved very quickly in recent years. It is, therefore, necessary to constantly renew and improve the skills of data scientists. For example, the eruption of bots and artificial intelligence mechanisms is revolutionizing the job, by integrating voice and images. Another example is the blockchain that revolutionizes the world of transactions by eliminating third parties and increasing the volume of processed data. Basically, it is more than necessary to hire only data scientists ready to revisit their skills with a very high frequency.

To Do!

The evolution of technologies requires an evolution of the jobs. On the one hand, do not underestimate the impact of a cloud project, on the other hand, anticipate the stakes by training existing staff and bringing in the organization these new profiles that will help you take advantage of these technologies. The cloud and data scientist specialists, among others, are the SEO specialists and community managers of the Internet, they ensure the optimum functioning of your investment. Do not neglect their importance or their skills!

Conclusion

We have come to the end of this chapter on best practices. I would like to stress the fact that the seven best practices shared here are neither panaceas nor options (or nice-to-haves). All successful cloud projects that I have had the chance to participate in have incorporated all these practices to a greater or lesser depth.

It is both these practices, often new, and their implementations that make cloud projects new, complex and exciting. If you've come this far, you're probably wondering if the game is worth the effort? The project looks monstrous. You were told that the cloud was simple, it was the solution to all your problems, that you were going to make huge savings. And now I'm breaking all your hopes. I put in front you of an Everest to climb without oxygen.

No revolution was made without "blood and tears," to paraphrase Churchill. If the cloud is the beginning of the fourth industrial revolution, we are only at the start of the technological roller coaster. So what can be expected from the digital transformation started by cloud technologies? That is what we will see in the next chapter. Articulated around the four axes of any organization: its customers (or citizens when it comes to public organizations), its employees, its operations and its business model, this chapter will allow you to understand the opportunities brought by the cloud.

6. Opportunities

« Ah! Human, this prodigy, resistant to his chances and fascinated by the scaffold of his vanities, continually quartered between what he believes to be and what he would like to be, forgetting that the simplest way to exist is to simply remain oneself. »

The African equation, Yasmina Khadra

If the cloud is certainly a set of technologies for the future, it is above all an opportunity for organizations to review their functioning and development. We saw in the previous chapters that the cloud increases agility, decreases IT costs, but also if not mainly, radically changes the management of an organization.

The cloud has given birth to new businesses and allowed them to grow, and to become real empires. We think of Netflix, Uber or Bitcoins, to name a few. However, a major part of these startups exists only because the cloud, its data centers, and its phenomenal computing power were available. Amazon, among others, by providing these entrepreneurs with massive data centers has enabled the emergence of these startups without the need to resort to hefty hardware and software investments. The power lies in their workforce and in their ability to invent economic models based on this intelligence.

This is one of the reasons why it is often said that data is the new oil; That these data are of a capital importance and value to who knows to use them. What is called information and communication technologies, and their existence in the cloud, is only a means to the service of an organization. We do not embrace the cloud because it is fashionable. I remain intimately convinced that the cloud is not the panacea and that every organization can find answers to its development without necessarily going to the cloud. However, this channel, this evolution, this transition will happen.

Just look at what happened to power generation or food. Just over a hundred and fifty years ago, electricity generation was usually the result of individuals who needed it for their business. Each plant had its own power generator. Then the idea of mutualizing this production appeared and electricity has gradually become a shared good. Thomas Edison established the first power station in 1882 in New York. It worked with coal and distributed a continuous current of one hundred and ten volts. This was before the start of the war between AC and DC, which ended in favor of the alternating current and gave birth to the first industrial conglomerate dedicated to electrical production: General Electric.

Similarly, when countries were mostly agricultural, food production was the result of small farmers who produced primarily for their own consumption and bartered the products of their farms. Then, little by little, the peasants abandoned their land to go to work in the city and in the twentieth century the agro-food industry became the first purveyor of food. Again, a pooling of the means of production.

The pooling of computer resources began with outsourcing in the nineties, accelerated over the last twenty years with the cloud and the development of the Internet. Resisting to it at any price is illusory. There will always be hardcore fighters, however, the fourth industrial revolution is here to stay.

So why the cloud? Why is it a revolution? First, because it affects all the elements of an organization, internal and external, jobs and processes. Then, because it redefines the edges of the organization, it makes them porous to interactions. Finally, because it modifies the governance models and influences the "business model". Some examples?

- The emergence of the drive-in supermarkets had been made possible only by the implementation of cloud technologies allowing the consumer to make his choices, order and pay for his purchases online before physically picking them, rather than paying a delivery. A hybrid distribution model.
- The rise of online banks was only possible by opening the data centers of the traditional banks. It is no longer a matter of a few employees running the transactions requested by the customers, but they do it themselves from any device connected to the Internet.
- The emergence of the sharing economy. Whether it is sharing an apartment, a car or a toolbox, there is a service that allows to connect supply and demand, sometimes without the exchange of money, but only through barter.
- Finally, the transformation of some hardware manufacturer/vendor business, to manufacturer/service provider of equipment formerly sold, using electronic and big data.

I could obviously multiply the examples. However, let's go together on a journey. The exciting and rich promises of the digital transformation of organizations organized around three themes:

- The transformation of customer/citizen engagement. How the cloud transforms the relationship with those who are at the center of the purpose of the organization;
- The transformation of work and of employee/work relationship. How the cloud changes the work and forces the jobs to evolve;
- The transformation of the organization and its governance model. How the cloud forces organizations to reinvent themselves.

Engaging customers/citizens

The customers of a commercial enterprise, the users of a public service and the citizens of a state are the reason for these organizations. Without customers and the income they bring, the company cannot live. Without users, the concept of "public" service disappears. Without citizens, there is no need to have a state.

The customer-organization relationship[51], in the broad sense, has evolved considerably over the last twenty years, mainly because of social networks and the speed with which the information is now circulating:

- Product evaluation and real-time shared customer reviews have a direct impact on their sales.
- The knowledge and analysis of customer transactions allow communicating effectively with customers. For example, a public office can send a reminder for a passport renewal before it expires. If the subscription to a magazine does not necessarily have an impact on a customer who can always get the last edition at a local bookstore, the story may be different for the passport that has expired and that may prevent the traveler from making the trip he planned.
- The knowledge and analysis of customer transactions enable effective cross-selling strategies to be put in place. It is for example accepted that product recommendation appearing at the bottom of the pages of Amazon (customers who bought this product also bought these) generate about ten percent of its turnover!
- The knowledge and analysis of customer transactions, linked to their behavior on social networks, allow to refine business models and to create even more personalized profiles, bringing the customer closer to the company, thanking him for its loyalty and developing its membership to a community of happy few (which are in fact a few million).

---

[51] For a question of simplification, I loosely use the term customer. A customer is usually the word used to designate the legal or physical person who buys products or services from a business. I also use it to designate the citizen who interacts with an administration. Thus, a citizen going to the passport office to renew her passport is the customer of this office, even if she does not buy anything, she uses the services. It is certain that I may offend some people by merging both words, the fact is that the concepts of customer service and quality of service are increasingly applied to public services, as they are in the commercial space.

From customer relationship...

The relationship between the seller and the customer has been theorized, dissected and analyzed from every angle. There is a plethora of books, training, and websites on how to increase sales, the art of selling, how to make customers happy, influence and manipulation, and so on.

However, nothing has more changed the customer relationship than what has been called the web 2.0, i.e. this internet revolution that allowed customers to express themselves and thus to be able to directly influence products, services, and shopping experience. Comments, blogs, communities and social networks allowed the client to take back some of the power that the brands were developing. It was therefore normal for brands to take on these tools to promote their products and especially, to try to manage these communities.

In twenty years, the customer relationship has thus shifted from a one-sided relationship of the seller to the customer to a bilateral relationship in which the customer's voice is expressed and influences the seller. This also allows the seller to increase her visibility, her sales and her return on investment in several ways, for example:

- Create and manage communities of ambassadors who will promote the products and services of a brand at a massively lower cost to those of conventional marketing;
- Launch, measure and adapt marketing campaigns in real time to increase the impact on the chosen target;
- Use the beta test concept (have the ambassadors test a new product) to improve a product before launching it with a wider target;
- Measure in real time the sentiment of users of a product and service based on social networks feeds like Twitter, Facebook, Instagram ...

The previous examples are only possible thanks to cloud technologies. If your IT is confined to your own four walls, you cannot execute any of these strategies.

...to seller relationship

The customer relationship of the twenty-first century is, therefore, that of a customer who expresses himself to a seller who listens ... and adapts. And it's win-win! What for? How? 3 simple reasons (but not necessarily easy to implement if you are only at the very beginning of your transition to the cloud, I am detailing this in Chapter 7, What do we do now?)

1. The creation and care of brand aficionados, which we call ambassadors, allow you to promote your products, to get rid of the famous consumer panel, and to test new products. Results: You increase the loyalty of your customers and you reduce your costs of testing and promoting products. How? Creating online communities, using chat rooms on your website where customers are first guided to your ambassadors, accessing product managers by integrating and federating your business directories.

2. By testing the campaigns in real time, you can automatically adapt the four Ps of the product mix: Price, Positioning, Promotion, and Packaging for maximum influence. Amazon, for example, does it admirably by adapting practically in real time the price of the products you have set aside in your wish lists to push you to purchase, to run its stock. Results: You pay less, and the seller sells its products. How? Creation of several simultaneous campaigns (visuals, targets, packaging, prices), the real-time return of data, analysis thanks to big data tools, automatic integration of results in the product mix and continuous analysis by artificial intelligence engines.

3. By measuring, responding and influencing sentiment analysis on social networks. Results: Customers feel listened to and you increase their loyalty. How? By defining the keywords, tags and ambassadors to follow and using a sentiment analysis engine, then allowing to respond either automatically by chatbots, or manually by web hosts or your ambassadors.

In the three cases above, you need to:

- Open your collaborative tools (email, file sharing, instant or persistent messaging, intranet) to ambassadors;
- Open your web business systems to the results defined by AI engines, which usually only work in cloud mode;
- Open your databases to link them to sentiment analyses to power the AI engines;

- Open your marketing systems to integrate campaign returns and provide leads to your business departments.

If you want to create this bilateral relationship between customers and sellers, it is important to define the interfaces and exchanges between the cloud systems and those that remain in your datacenter.

The story of Carlo's Bakery, in the United States, as reported by SalesForce.com[52] is interesting from the point of view of the evolution of its customer relationship. Starting from a century-old family bakery in New Jersey, Carlo's Bakery has become a franchise that not only manufactures more than twenty-four thousand cupcakes a week but exports them worldwide, while continuing to be close to its customers, with a local touch.

The advantage of an SME, compared to a large industrial group, is its flexibility and the lack of existing computing power. It is then simpler to start with a cloud solution to build its electronic customer relationship. One of the main points, in this case, is the existence of several points of sale distant from each other and from the headquarters of the company.

With a star or mesh configuration, maintaining a centralized proprietary system is costly and can be complex in terms of security. With a cloud-based system, it is possible to share elastic resources by managing a simple and secure Internet connection, while preserving the possibility of increasing or reducing the use of resources according to the quirks of the company's development.

In addition, the use of a centralized cloud computing system allows leveraging additional services that you "just" need to activate, such as data analysis, encryption or sentiment analysis to name a few, without undergoing their development or operating costs. I put "just" between quotation marks because marketing tends to make things simple. If it is true that you must "just" decide to use a service to access it, its actual usage is not usually as simple as it seems. This often requires reflection, preparation, and adaptation of the systems. The fact is, it usually remains faster and easier to implement than a local system that requires hardware, software, and service.

---

[52] https://www.salesforce.com/customer-success-stories/carlos-bakery/

If the success of the Online CRM is no longer to be demonstrated, however, it is only the tip of the cloud computing iceberg. The real intelligence is divided between linking data from heterogeneous systems and the utilization of the information that is derived. It is from this use that the transformation of the organization-customer relationship is born, and to ensure that the latter is listened to and feels concerned and can act faster and better.

Services to connect

To achieve a renewed and personalized interaction between customers and sellers, citizens and civil servants, several systems must be assembled, as illustrated in Figure 6-1 - Implementing a new customer relationship.

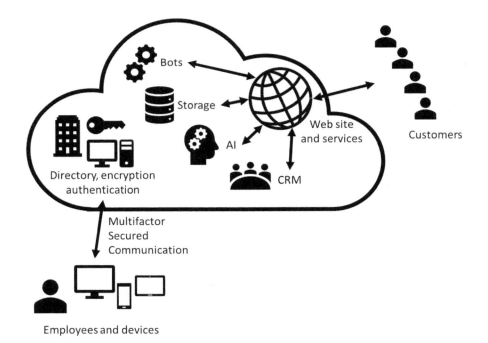

Figure 6-1 - Implementing a new customer relationship

Each cloud service provider has its own bill of materials, not always easy to decipher. The Table 6-1 - Name of services among the main suppliers allows you to quickly view the services to be implemented to transform this relationship. This list is not exhaustive and constantly evolving. At the time of writing this book, some services were still in beta mode.

Service	Microsoft	Amazon	Google
Directory	Active Directory Azure	Amazon Cloud Directory AWS Directory Service Amazon Cognitive	Google Cloud IAM Cloud Identity-Aware Proxy
Security	Active Directory Azure Multi-factor Authentication	AWS IAM AWS Certificate Manager AWS Key Management Service	Security Key Enforcement Cloud Key Management Service
CRM	Dynamics 365		
The	Machine Learning Azure Analysis Service Many API voice, vision ...	Amazon Machine Learning	Cloud Machine Learning Engine Many API voice, vision ...
Storage	SQL Database SQL Data warehouse Azure Cosmos DB Data Lake Store	Amazon Aurora Amazon RDS Amazon DynamoDB Amazon RedShift	Cloud SQL Cloud Spanner Cloud Bigtable Cloud Datastore
Bots	Azure bots service	Amazon Lex	
Web Site	Virtual Machines APP Service Media Service Cloud Services	Amazon EC2 AWS Elastic Beanstalk Auto Scaling AWS Mobile Hub	Compute Engine Cloud Load Balancing

Table 6-1 - Name of services among the main suppliers

You get the impression by looking at Table 6-1 that service providers do everything to maintain confusion. The names of the services are different but do not always reflect the same underlying reality. It is a different philosophy. Microsoft revolves around Active Directory, Hyper-V, and SQL Server, its cloud services are strongly marked by its on-premises software history. Google and Amazon are "pure players" that have first built these services for their own needs before they marketed and made them a full-fledged business. No worries to have though, but just take your time to fully understand how those bricks fit together, integrate and extend your existing infrastructure.

I would, however, note that if on paper the solution is elegant and looks simple, it requires some serious implementation, especially with AI and bots. The proposed tools are not intrinsically intelligent. They allow developing a form of intelligence, provided you go through a learning phase which can be long and laborious.

If the "external" relationship of the organization seems naturally attracted to the cloud, what about its "internals" with its employees?

Increase employee collaboration and engagement

There is a strong bet that if you read this book, you have a smartphone, a tablet or a computer, or even the three. If this is the case, you may have a personal email account, hosted by your ISP or at one of the major vendors such as Gmail, Outlook.com or Yahoo. It is also very possible for you to consult this mailbox from the three electronic devices mentioned above, no matter where you are, as long as you have an Internet connection. There is also a strong bet that you read the press online on these devices, order products or services, check your bank account, declare your taxes, etc. In doing so, you consume cloud services, almost without realizing it!

What about your company? Can you read and send your professional emails on your phone, safely? Can you access a customer's information while you're on the move? Can you file your expense report without going to the company headquarters? Can you organize an audio or video conference with your colleagues while you are in a hotel abroad? If this is the case for one or more of these applications, is it simple and economical?

If you cannot do it or if the procedures are complex and the costs are high, it is very likely that cloud computing has not yet reached your organization. It is possible that questions of security, regulation or simply reluctance are at the root of these impossibilities. However, going to the cloud will bring incredible benefits in terms of fluidity, collaboration and security to the organization.

Messaging

Email has become a basic service for any employee. Keeping an e-mail server on-premises is equivalent to producing its own electricity (except if you are a player in the electricity grid, but this is another discussion). Transferring mail to the cloud will have four major advantages:

1. No hardware to manage, no mailbox size saturation and whatnot directly related to the hardware.
2. Universal access, anywhere on any device.
3. Increased security, especially in terms of malware and access. No patches to apply to servers, no anti-virus signatures to update constantly, a decrease or even a disappearance of spam, ransomware, phishing, among others.
4. An invoice per mailbox that allows charging each department for the services it consumes.

Messaging should be one of the first services to outsource, with no other question to ask. Obviously, security and confidentiality are to be considered, go back to Chapter 5, Best practices.

Document sharing

Some files may not be, or should not be, attached to e-mail messages, for security, confidentiality, or size issues. One of the ways to avoid attachments is to use a file sharing system like Dropbox, OneDrive or Google Drive. No more saturation of mailboxes or managing multiple versions and copies of the same document.

In addition, document-sharing management systems often allow you to work simultaneously on the same document and to apply advanced security rules.

Instant Messaging

WhatsApp, Skype, Messenger or Snap are on all phones of the "millennials" and many other people. These applications allow you to communicate quickly in writing, video or audio with one or more correspondents. In addition, communications can be persistent. Each correspondent can have its status, updated manually or automatically, to be able to be contacted.

Some of these services, such as Skype, allow you to extend communications to phone numbers. It is then possible to have a single communication interface (either software or hardware) for all text, voice and video communications. It is a question of integrating telephone and computer networks to pass all communications on the latter. In doing so, you can envisage a decrease in telephone costs, all calls between employees, whether they are inside or outside the corporate network, passing through an IP network.

Real-Time Collaboration

If you have not yet heard about HipChat, Slack or Microsoft teams, you will soon. These tools of "team messaging" or real-time collaboration are spreading. They are a fusion of the previous three, in persistent and collaborative mode. Confused? Imagine working with a group of people on the same project. You will exchange communications, share files and make meetings. So instead of using different tools, let's integrate them into one.

These tools are not limited to messaging, document sharing and communication. They have opening points to other tools that they can integrate, like OneNote, Twitter, SurveyMonkey, etc. The first idea is to make this application the first destination of team collaboration.

Mobility

One of the strengths of the previous tools is their existence on all mobile platforms. A tool like Skype for Business exists on Windows, MacOS, IOS, and Android. It is then possible, with a single Internet connection, to homogenize the working modes irrespective of the device used and the place where the employees are located.

This hypermobility also has its setbacks as it becomes possible to work anywhere at any time. The labor law in France, in force since January 1, 2017 also recognizes a "right to disconnect".

Security and privacy

One of the first reservations about cloud services is data security and privacy. However, as we have seen in all previous chapters, the security of data stored in a private or public cloud is often greater than it might be in a local datacenter. The same is true of privacy, which is generally guaranteed by strict controls and respect for local regulations.

On the other hand, the use of the cloud allows the implementation of additional security mechanisms that increase the software's robustness of mobile devices and reduce the risk of loss or theft of data. As we have seen in Chapter 5, Best Practices, the cloud enables the implementation of encryption, multifactor authentication, documents rights management, application of software patches, testing of hyperlinks and attachments, to name but a few of security features that sometimes are "just" to be activated[53].

Collaboration, decision, and commitment

I could multiply the examples of cloud applications that will allow employees to be more efficient, more productive and make better decisions based on facts and coherent data rather than the goodwill of a fraction of people. There is as much to bet as the months and years to come you bring us their lot of changes to start with the integration of more and more big data and artificial intelligence.

However, one of the points I have, personally, experienced using modern tools of collaboration is their appropriation! By this I mean that when a tool is perceived to bring a real added value, the employees take ownership of it quickly and begin to disseminate it in their personal sphere, thereby gaining fluidity of use. The organization then reinforces its image of innovation and champion of productivity, gaining a greater commitment of employees.

There is, however, the risk of perverse effects that of further blurring the boundary between work and personal life. Hence the "right to disconnect" from the French labor law. However, the implementation of cloud technologies within the organization is fortunate to be able to be accompanied and supervised by the Human Resources department. As I like to repeat: if the organization does not provide you with the tools to be productive and do your job as best as possible, employees will find the means that suit them and there

---

[53] I'm putting "just" between quotation marks to insist that if the technical factor is simple to implement in the cloud, the human factor is the one that will make its implementation successful or not. It is therefore appropriate as we have seen in Chapter 5, Best Practices, to prepare and accompany the change.

is an even greater risk that this is not the best regarding security, privacy, and integrity of data, applications, and usage.

New needs, new jobs

If the cloud transforms the collaboration and commitment of the employees, it also transforms the jobs, as we have seen in Chapter 5, Best Practices. New ones appear, existing ones evolve and sometimes disappear.

Let's have a look at call centers and customer relationship management. The bots and AI will revolutionize these jobs, as the answering machine has made redundant the person in charge of picking the phone and dispatching the calls. Already today, many bots allow limiting the number of calls to technical support requiring this fact less personnel. At the same time, it is necessary to integrate those bots, to define their vocabulary, their heuristics and limits. This requires special skills to be acquired.

We will see next the management of the digital communities that get created and is the changing role of the community manager. One can also mention the need to integrate cloud technologies with the existing ones that requires specific skills to be acquired by the IT team. The sales and business management will require big data specialists with dual skills: business and IT. Again, I can multiply the examples. The point on which I wish to insist is that all the jobs of any company are affected. This requires a great coordination between human resources (or human capital as we tend to call it now), IT and business, in order to define the necessary changes and adaptations. It is only at this price that the organization will be able to modernize itself and take advantage of the new developments to come.

Services to connect

When you see how fast some solutions like Basecamp[54] or Slack[55] have grown, you realize that the use of collaboration and productivity tools in the cloud is not only a reality, it is obvious. Ubiquity, ease, and speed are the direct benefits of these solutions.

---

[54] https://basecamp.com/
[55] https://slack.com/

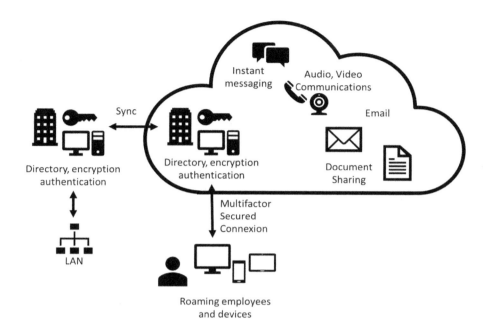

Figure 6-2 - Collaboration and productivity in the cloud

Transferring all the productivity tools to the cloud certainly requires increased bandwidth and connection reliability. However, the benefits in terms of access, security, and management are, as previously seen, instantaneous.

However, there is still a significant challenge from the relative hegemony of Microsoft on the productivity sector. Tools like Office, Exchange or SharePoint have become almost standard over the years. Not that this is a bad thing as the quality of their products have improved in recent times, but some companies are reluctant to depend on a single provider for their collaboration infrastructure.

You will find in Table 6-2 - Collaborative Solutions in the cloud A list of cloud services offered by major suppliers and other smaller ones. As we will see in the next part of this chapter, Transform your organization, the existence of the cloud has allowed the budding of a multitude of startups in almost all areas. In fact, there is a wide range of cloud solutions that meet various collaboration and communication needs.

The list of Table 6-2 is not exhaustive. But it illustrates a part of the vast choice that exists.

Service	Microsoft	Amazon	Google	Autres
Messaging	Exchange Online Office 365	Amazon WorkMail	Gmail G Suite	IBM Verse Zimbra Collaboration Kolab
Instant Messaging	Skype company Online	Amazon Chime	Hangouts G Suite	IBM Connections Zimbra Talk
Persistent Messaging	Teams (Office 365)			Slack HipChat Workgroup
Audio, video calls	Skype Enterprise Online	Amazon Chime	Hangouts	IBM Connections Zimbra Talk
Document sharing	OneDrive Enterprise SharePoint Online Office	Amazon WorkDocs	Google Drive Google Docs	IBM Connections Zimbra Collaboration Kolab
Social network	Yammer		Google+	Workplace (Facebook) Drupal

Table 6-2 - Collaborative Solutions in the cloud

Two key points to consider when adopting a collaboration tool: authentication and adherence to standards. Authentication, because it is the basis of all security. Multiply the identities of the users and you open Pandora's box of the human provoked security faults and an increase in support calls (loss of password is the number one reason for support calls). Respect for standards, because between PCI DSS in the financial sector, GDPR In Europe and many others, the use of several independent services can harm the beautiful building that is necessary to maintain compliance to any to legal obligations.

We still need to have a look at how cloud technologies will help you change your organization and transform it upside down.

Transform your organization

In 2016, Klaus Schwab, the founder of the Davos Forum, introduced the term "Fourth Industrial Revolution" to talk about the increased presence of new technologies. Many companies have since embraced this notion. If I am not here to enumerate the industrial revolutions and decide between Jeremy Rifkin, the father of the third, and Klaus Schwab, it has been clear for the last ten years that digital technologies and the cloud, driven by mobile tech, are revolutionizing the world.

> **Note** The world has started to move to all-digital with crypto-currencies. If the phenomena of Bitcoin and blockchain are not at the origin of this digital evolution, they are poised to become its foundation and revolutionize society and organizations much more in-depth than did the three previous industrial revolutions.

If we can question the valorization of many unicorns, these start-ups worth more than a billion dollars, they have, for many, changed entire industrial sectors, without having real tangible assets. Netflix did not have a data center and had no content before it started to produce it. Airbnb has no data center, no hotel and yet is worth more than Marriott, Starwood or Accor. Uber is worth more than Hertz without owning any car. If you find dozens of business examples that do not exist without the cloud, the latter is one of the ways to transform any organization.

What a start-up does today without owning any servers or software, any organization is technically capable of doing it. I say technically because as we have seen before, there are many curbs, real or perceived, cultural, legal or organizational, to the cloud. Here are some reflections, starting from real examples of possible digital transformations.

Uberization

The term, introduced in 2014 by Maurice Levy, former CEO of Publicis, in an interview given to the Financial Times[56], derived from the Uber company, and has its Wikipedia page[57] Since those last two years. Uberization and

---

[56] https://www.ft.com/content/377f7054-81ef-11e4-b9d0-00144feabdc0
[57] https://en.wikipedia.org/wiki/Uberisation

disintermediation are terms that are frequently encountered. Any company is in fact at risk of getting obsolete by a new player changing the rules of the game by introducing a new business model. Hotels made obsolete by renting apartments between individuals thanks to Airbnb? Not totally but put at risk for sure and forced to react.

The "uberization" is based on mobile, broadband internet and various services, such as geo-location, image or character recognition. It is also characterized by a greater simplification of the proposed service: greater responsiveness, online payment, and service evaluation. Without going into the social, legal and fiscal issues of the phenomenon of the uberization, let's look at how to adapt those concepts to existing organizations.

Note Many start-ups like Uber consume capital without, for a long time, making a profit. This is a risk to be considered by any organization that wants to position itself with flexible services of this type. However, what is put forward here is the approach of using an essential aspect of these start-ups: the cloud. Those companies can only exist by using cloud digital capabilities that do not belong to them. This is also the availability of these capabilities by Amazon, via Amazon Web Services, which originally enabled the emergence of these start-ups.

The first question to ask is whether the organization can be uberized? Is it possible to be "disintermediated"? There is also a chance (a risk) that this is already happening. It is then necessary to take the lead and to uberize oneself, by developing a new approach (why not another brand to not cannibalize the existing one) exclusively based on mobile tools and cloud.

The second question to answer is to compare the pros and cons of uberized services versus those who are not. It is not all about cost. This is one aspect of Uber, but not the only one. Availability, information, and quality are to be considered. It is also a great way to improve existing services by adding this uberization touch.

The availability of services raises the question of redundancy and universal access. With cloud services, these two characteristics become intrinsic. The availability of information allows transparency, a majority of customers/citizens wants to know what is going on behind the scenes, who we are dealing with, or understand the procedure. Quality can be evaluated on the fly by an immediate survey system. But it is primarily in the use of data that the most important benefits will appear. The collection and analysis of the data allow to really measure the different dimensions of the service provided and to propose improvements. After ubiquity, it is the "big data" that will be the source of the evolution of the services offered.

Things, complexity, and forecast

One of the heavy trends of the last few years is the Internet of Things (IoT). If some industries have used sensors for many years, the revolution comes from their connection to the Internet. Sending data continuously, these sensors help detect a failure before it arrives, correct a deviation before it has negative consequences or simply establish basic systems comprehension.

These "things" are increasingly present, less and less expensive and can use their own low-bandwidth and low-consumption internet. Gartner estimates that there will be twenty-six billion connected objects by 2020. So, if privacy (it becomes possible to spy on everyone permanently), environmental impact (all these objects are electronic) or security (these objects are potentially hackable) questions arise, the potential of the transformation of organizations is immense.

Of course, many hurdles remain, especially due to the lack of standards in this emerging economic pan. The networks used, LoRa, M2M, Sigfox, are not compatible with each other. The format of the sent message is not standardized, just to mention two of those obstacles. However, the development of interfaces and middleware allows to quickly bypass them and deploy a mesh of objects.

It is beyond the object that its utility and its power appear. Let's imagine a factory with robots, power tools, and many workers. We will find hundreds of sensors and connected objects or even thousands. Let's say, for our demonstration, there are two thousand. Each of these sensors sends out every two seconds, a message of one hundred and forty bytes (a special tweet). If this plant operates with two shifts, or sixteen hours a day, our two thousand sensors generate seven point five gigabytes (7.5 GB) of data per day. If you find this huge, do the following calculation: 2,000 sensors times 140 bytes times 30 per minute times 16 hours per day (2,000 x 140 x 30 x 60 x 16 = 8,064,000,000 bytes).

Not only are you going to need storage (2.68 terabytes per year), but you're going to need to do something with this data, both in real time for those that return critical and timely data to find causalities and correlations, in order to transform this data into information. The key to success of the Internet of Things.

By analyzing the movement of elevators in a high-rise building, the passenger flow and the waiting period, the company ThyssenKrupp allowed innovating by putting two cabs in the same shaft[58]. But it is by using the Internet of Things that ThyssenKrupp has transformed a part of his business and the maintenance of these elevators[59]. This not only provides a better diagnosis in case of breakdown, by aggregating all the failures and solutions of all the elevators (knowledge base augmented by artificial intelligence) but above all to make predictions and to step in before a failure occurs, planning more precisely and thereby limiting downtime. This was made possible using cloud systems, allowing the connection of a large sensor network and analysis of the generated data.

The capture of object data, their analysis, the discovery of inferences and the learning of models as time progresses, allow to preempt the incidents and to refine the forecasts. A bit of Minority Report adapted to the industry.

Target, analyze and correct

There was the "data analyst" and there was the "data scientist". The difference between the two? The first is usually in charge of analyzing a data source, the second of several. The first one uses simple heuristics, the second complex ones. The first one is laborious, the second adventurous. All this is a bit of a caricature but illustrates that the data has become critical and that the cloud offers analysis tools that becomes difficult and costly to run locally.

---

[58] https://www.thyssenkruppelevator.com/elevator-products/twin
[59] https://blogs.microsoft.com/firehose/2014/07/16/the-internet-of-things-gives-the-worlds-cities-a-major-lift/

Unilever North America wanted to improve the performance of its marketing campaigns. While all its data was local, it was not only difficult to correlate them, but also to spread internationally. Using cloud technologies[60], the company was able to reduce the time it took to create a campaign from two weeks to two days. It can also in quasi-real-time change the settings of a campaign if it does not give the desired results. It can also test a campaign on a country and replicate it in case of success to others much faster than it could have done before.

This is an example, among many others, of the power, the flexibility and the speed that becomes possible with the cloud. One of the aspects to consider is the cost of processing these data. But overall, the cloud makes four things more difficult to do locally:

1. Aggregate data from multiple silos. The important thing is to be able to put its data in relation. It is generally necessary to use extraction, transformation and loading tools (ETL) to store the data in a warehouse. Using the cloud makes it possible to access virtually unlimited space at a low cost, with top security and redundancy.
2. Query this data to find relationships. Anyone who has done a bit of data analysis knows that the size of a data warehouse can quickly become exponential and as a result, the queries can become very slow. The use of Big Data technologies from, such as the *High-Performance Computing*, then becomes necessary to reduce wait times.
3. Use inference engines to make predictions. "Machine learning" requires power and intelligence. The machine will learn from heuristics that we have programmed and that we can adapt. All major cloud service providers offer forecasting tools, which the "data scientist" will use for trend detection and enable predictive model implementation.
4. Switch to real time. With the forecast models in place, with the flow of data being channeled, it becomes possible to analyze the data continuously and to detect exceptional events in real time, such as behavioral deviations in the data models, by minimizing false positives.

---

[60] https://aws.amazon.com/solutions/case-studies/unilever/

It quickly becomes possible to choose a target (customers, prospects, populations, etc.), to test its models on this target, to analyze the results in real time and to correct if necessary. As in the example of Unilever, the benefits are shortened time, reduced costs and indirectly increased reliability of results.

Try, fail, start over

In March 2012, the Washington Post headline read *The new #Fail: Fail fast, fail early and fail often* (with the hashtag, popularized by Twitter to define keywords)[61]. The article opens with this sentence: "The future of innovation is in learning how to fail".

However, if innovation is often synonymous with repeated failures, it comes at a cost. As Edison said about the invention of the electric bulb: "I have not failed. I just found 10,000 solutions that do not work." Except that the 10,000 unsuccessful tests cost time and money. We now know how to model complex physical phenomena. Planes, for example, are entirely computer-designed with increased reliability even before the first models and the first actual flights.

But it is in the digital world that the "fail fast" is prevailing. All software vendors now offer their creations in beta format. Not just for users to test them, but to collect usage and satisfaction data. They can then know what works and what does not. They can test a feature and make it evolve over time.

However, to be able to do it on a global scale, a cloud infrastructure is required. How can we make a single application available to millions of users on the planet? Only the cloud allows it, at controlled costs and with short reaction times. The model can then be replicated to all industrial sectors. Tesla does it with all his cars, to the point that the industry is now following. Commercial jets are now connected configurable machines.

I was talking recently with the IT manager of an airline that was going to receive new Airbus A350s. It was the first aircraft that the company received for which IT was a part of the receiving protocol. The airplane is indeed connected which

---

[61] https://www.washingtonpost.com/blogs/innovations/post/the-new-fail-fail-fast-fail-early-and-fail-often/2012/05/30/gJQAKA891U_blog.html?utm_term=.9ada82ef4396

puts IT management at the center of the operations. In addition, this aircraft is powered by Rolls-Royce, a leading cloud technology company, relying on Microsoft Azure to provide real-time information to maintenance engineers to reduce downtime[62].

It is, therefore, possible to develop a new product or service, to have it tested, to analyze the data and to be able to decide whether it should be launched or not. It will therefore no longer be necessary to try 10,000 solutions that do not work, but a much smaller number, before finding the one we were looking for.

Services to connect

Compute power, storage and access to cognitive services (voice and video recognition, on-the-fly translation, inference engines, forecasting, etc.) make the cloud a must-have like running water or electricity. The Figure 6-3 - Cloud services for the transformation of organizations suggests some services to connect to access this power.

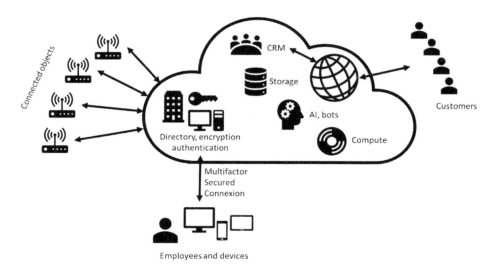

Figure 6-3 - Cloud services for the transformation of organizations

If the two previous parts of this chapter were relatively open in terms of competition. The latter which implements very advanced services is the turf of

---

[62] https://customers.microsoft.com/en-US/story/rollsroycestory

the very large suppliers, as you can see in Table 6-3 - Services dedicated to the transformation of your organization. This table, like the ones that preceded, is not exhaustive, especially in the world of connected objects that is in full effervescence and still looking for common standards. But it gives you a first idea of the advanced services available in the cloud.

Service	Microsoft	Amazon	Google	Other
CRM	Dynamics 365			Salesforce.com
IA	Machine Learning Azure Analysis Service Many voice API, vision…	Amazon Machine Learning	Cloud Machine Learning Engine Many API voice, vision …	IBM Watson
Storage	SQL Database SQL Data Warehouse Azure Cosmos DB Data Lake Store	Amazon Aurora Amazon RDS Amazon DynamoDB Amazon RedShift	Cloud SQL Cloud Spanner Cloud Bigtable Cloud Datastore	IBM Bluemix
Bots	Azure bots service	Amazon Lex		
Compute	Virtual Machines App Service Virtu AzureaL Machine Scale Set	Amazon EC2 AWS Batch Auto Scaling AWS Mobile Hub	Compute Engine APP Engine Cloud Load Balancing	IBM Bluemix
Connected objects	IoT Hub IoT Edge Event Hubs Event Grid	AWS Platform IoT AWS Greengrass Bouton AWS IoT	Cloud IoT Core	IBM Watson IoT Orange Live Objects Objenious

Table 6-3 - Services dedicated to the transformation of your organization

As with all the services we have encountered over these pages, these advanced services allow all actors, including SOHOs, to have access to an impossible power some time ago. It is possible to run powerful predictive models for a few dollars where millions were needed to acquire super calculators a few years back. Same for connected objects. If the lack of a standard is a deterrent, the existence of connection platforms offered by all the major players allows the creation of networks of heterogeneous objects in a few clicks and a few lines of code. The real revolution is there and it will transform our future and that of all organizations.

If I have managed to convince you and you are still with me, we have the last chapter to go through. Certainly, the most important! Act!

Opportunities

7. What do we do now?

« What would be in the end if everything was in the beginning? »

Notre-Dame de Paris, Victor Hugo

If for me, the question of the cloud is now irrelevant, it remains nebulous (pun intended) for the average person. Of course, everyone with a computer or smartphone uses the cloud without knowing it. But in an organization, it is another story. We have gone through the previous pages on the challenges concerning security, privacy, change management, etc. All this can scare and delay or kill any initiative.

A July 2017 article from the French newspaper Le Monde Informatique[63] revealed that nine out of ten digital transformation projects were doomed to fail. It's true that digital transformation is more ambitious than just the use of cloud technologies. However, the first step in any digital transformation is often

---

[63] http://www.lemondeinformatique.fr/actualites/lire-transformation-digitale-9-projects-on-10-you-a-l-chess-68938

the organization-wide use of the cloud. So how do you increase your chances of success?

The following pages are the result of nearly ten years of successes and failures to implement cloud technologies in various types of organizations, of any size and of any industry. But there is no miracle recipe. The marketing that continues promising the moon effortlessly is no more or less than deceptive advertising. The adoption of cloud technologies in a company that has a well-established and functional local IT infrastructure will never be total. There are many pitfalls. The good news is that they can be avoided. We met them in Chapter 5, Best Practices.

This last chapter focuses on the first few months, crucial to any project. Its goal is to define a simple plan for successful adoption of cloud technologies. As the saying goes, "It's not rocket science." There is nothing infinitely complicated or technically insurmountable. All aspects of the cloud need to be considered: technical, organizational, human and legal, from the outset of the project to understand all the limits, the benefits and the journey to be traveled. Ready? Let's go!

Where to start?

To this question, I generally answer "at the beginning". And this beginning is first the willingness to go to the cloud. You have this intuition that the cloud is the solution to all your problems. Stop for a few moments though! The cloud is not and will never be the solution to all your problems. As I like to repeat to my customers, the cloud is A solution, it is not THE solution. When I created my first professional electronic mailbox in 1993, I could not foresee that the number one method of communication fifteen years later would be e-mail. It was not at the time the solution to the communication problems between individuals and organizations. It is not the solution today, but one of the solutions. We understand this now, with the evolution of instant messaging, then group messaging, and WhatsApp or Snap.

Start with Why

Simon Sinek, a British author and speaker, has become famous thanks to his TED talk, how great leaders inspire action[64] (One of the twenty most seen episodes on the TED site), and his book Start with why. As the summary of this book indicates: "...people won't truly buy a product, service, movement, or idea until they understand the WHY behind".

The real answer to the question where to start is to actually answer another question: Why? Why the cloud, what are you looking to do, what objective to achieve? There are as many reasons to go to the cloud as there are individuals on this planet. But the why you do what you do, or in any case want to do what you want to do, and do it in the cloud is, in my humble opinion, the only important answer to the choice of the cloud.

We can group possible answers to why in four categories:

1. *Cost reduction*. It costs you too much money. Too many fixed assets, too expensive software and hardware prices, exorbitant operating costs ... This is often the number one reason that drives businesses to the cloud.
2. *Installing a new software solution*. You have a need and this one can be satisfied with a cloud solution.
3. *Refocusing on your core business*. IT has become a goal and not a means, it is time to set it to its place. By outsourcing this function, resources can be freed to refocus on the organization's mission.
4. *Increase in Its capabilities*. Whether it is the availability rate, or the services used, the goal is to do more, for the same or lesser costs.

Note A clear majority of cloud projects are initially costlier than their local counterparts. For two simple reasons: 1. The cost is a deceptive marketing argument that does not go the distance more than five minutes. 2. The human component is generally not or little considered and in fact, change management is very often much longer and more painful than expected.

---

[64] https://www.ted.com/talks/simon_sinek_how_great_leaders_inspire_action

This is the answer to why that will allow you to identify the project or solution to send to the cloud. The mistake would be to consider only a cloud solution though! The cloud is not always the solution, even if it is gradually imposed on all the projects and all the organizations. A SWOT analysis[65] (*Strength, Weakness, Opportunity, Threats*), a simple list of benefits and drawbacks, or even a complete *Business case* are all methods that can allow you to decide. If one of the primary motivations of the cloud is cost-cutting, the *buzzword* for some years in the computer world is Total Cost of Ownership, the famous TCO. Let's have a look.

Total Cost of Ownership

I often meet Customers who want to do a total cost of ownership study[66]. These are usually those that have nothing or few systems that work in cloud mode. Often inspired by the many studies that exist on the topic and the marketing campaign of the cloud providers, they want to know whether the publicized savings are real in their case.

Microsoft[67] and AWS[68], among others, provide calculation tools for the total cost of ownership of cloud solutions. Often developed with consulting firms, these tools are far from being unbiased but offer a good first idea of the cost differences between a local solution and its equivalent in the cloud. The two reports illustrated in the Figure 7-1 - Extract from the Microsoft Azure TCO report and Figure 7-2 - Extract from the Amazon Web Services TCO Report provide an overview of the result of the cloud setting of 10 quad-core four-processor servers, with 128 GB of memory, and a 10 TB SAN.

Both reports provide different results because the Amazon questionnaire does not consider the backup and archiving systems, which Microsoft requires. *So*, Microsoft removes the cost of these on-premises systems resulting in larger savings. Moreover, these tools are based on heuristics that do not necessarily

---

[65] https://en.wikipedia.org/wiki/SWOT_analysis
[66] https://en.wikipedia.org/wiki/Total_cost_of_ownership and https://en.wikipedia.org/wiki/Whole-life_cost
[67] http://tco.microsoft.com/
[68] https://aws.amazon.com/tco-calculator/

adapt to your reality, if only in relation to the accounting depreciation of your material or the cost of labor.

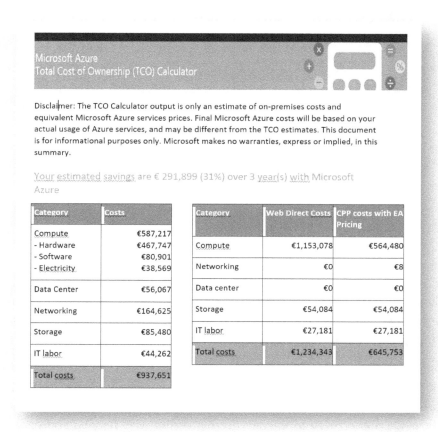

Figure 7-1 - Extract from the Microsoft Azure TCO report

There are also two costs that are generally systematically ignored by this type of study: the cost of migration and the training of IT teams. Yet, moving existing systems and applications to the cloud is not neutral and can be costly, especially if the applications have not natively been intended for the cloud. The training of IT teams can also be very costly, even if it can be seen as a necessary investment to adapt to the new realities of modern information systems.

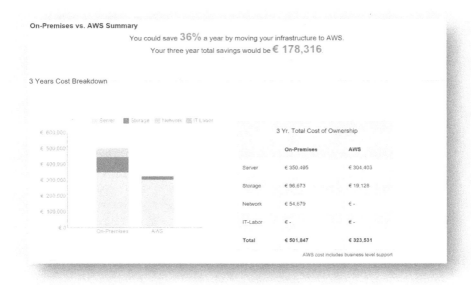

On-Premises vs. AWS Summary

You could save 36% a year by moving your infrastructure to AWS.
Your three year total savings would be € 178,316

3 Years Cost Breakdown

3 Yr. Total Cost of Ownership

	On-Premises	AWS
Server	€ 350,495	€ 304,403
Storage	€ 96,673	€ 19,128
Network	€ 54,679	€ -
IT-Labor	€ -	€ -
Total	€ 501,847	€ 323,531

AWS cost includes business level support

Figure 7-2 - Extract from the Amazon Web Services TCO Report

Finally, these studies are primarily marketing tools! It is therefore rare that they display a result that is against of what they promote. Even, if in the medium and long-term, it is generally agreed that the cloud carries real savings.

As a rule, the TCO studies offered by cloud service providers are a good start for comparing local and cloud technologies, but in no way can they replace a comprehensive cost study that takes into account all aspects of the project. They provide a good way to engage the discussion with finance and general management. They have the immense advantage of taking a different look at the cloud.

An important point to mention: depending on the accounting practices and the modes of operations in place in the organization, the passage to the cloud may lead to a passage of Capex to Opex. In other words, the end of the acquisition of hardware and software, and the beginning of their rental. This can be a means to reduce the use of capital and assets to increase operating costs. Many organizations have often already evolved into their practices by moving to the leasing of their equipment or by outsourcing the operations of their data centers.

Beyond finances

I will not come back to the other benefits of cloud solutions compared to local ones. We have met many of them in previous pages, including technical, organizational or functional. In your quest for the project to setup in cloud mode, these benefits are to be clearly described.

The acquisition and implementation of equipment are often at the top of the list of these benefits, particularly in emerging markets. Between obtaining a quotation and the actual implementation of the equipment, it may take several months. It is not unusual that between these two milestones, the recommended hardware no longer exists and must be replaced by other references. The range of equipment a manufacturer keeps is constantly evolving and has a very limited lifespan. With the cloud, a fraction of a second can happen between the quotation and the implementation. This speed can induce significant financial benefits, but also and above all psychological and organizational.

Imagine the implementation of a decision within a few days or the implementation of a new system in a few hours. In fact, this speed can be disturbing for many who will see it as a result of hasty decisions. Yet it is the paradigm shift that cloud technologies offer. Many decision makers and organizations do not realize the scope of this speed.

Every time I demonstrate or have demonstrated the creation of a virtual machine on a cloud platform, the connection of a mobile application and the tracking of the deployment of this application within a few minutes, I have received incredulous glances. Arthur Clarke, the author of 2001: A Space Odyssey, wrote: "Any sufficiently advanced technology is indistinguishable from magic"[69]. Sometimes this applies well to the cloud. Most of the new users find it just magical. A click and I have a fully functional and secure virtual machine. A

---

[69] This is in fact the third of "Clarke's three laws":
https://en.wikipedia.org/wiki/Clarke%27s_three_laws Not to be confused with the Three laws of robotics, formulated by Isaac Asimov:
https://en.wikipedia.org/wiki/Three_Laws_of_Robotics.

line of code and I link mobile and cloud service. An "upload" and I make available an application to millions of users around the world.

The cloud carries today this advantage of short time on the market. The startups have also well understood this, adopting Amazon's services to develop theirs[70]. Beyond financial considerations, it is this advantage that must be considered. Of course, the financial, security and organizational aspects are to be considered. Especially security, that becomes one of the main concerns of organizations and individuals. But this time to market is unmatched to date. Angry birds could not have been the planetary success that this game was without the cloud. Minecraft would have been able to grow as quickly as it had without the cloud. LinkedIn could not have become the number one of the professional social networks without the cloud. Refusing to see this reality today for any organization is the guarantee of becoming obsolete as quickly as the cloud becomes unavoidable.

But let's go back to business and our why! If you have found it or think you have found it, the second important step is to prove it. For this, nothing beats the famous POC, or Proof Of Concept.

Proof of concept

The Proof of concept is an important step on your path to the cloud. Be careful not to confuse proof of concept and pilot project, these are two totally different things. The proof of concept is short and should not be put into production. This is only a demonstration of the feasibility of the solution to a small group of users that has no impact on your production systems. If the proof of concept fails, then it is simple and quick to remove the tested service(s) without production being impacted in any way.

There are however three rules that I advise to respect for a successful proof of concept:

1. Choose a group of testers outside the IT department. Not that the IT department should not be involved. IT professionals tend to focus on

---

[70] I would advise the interview of Andy Jassy, CEO of AWS, by Ed Lazowska at the University of Washington. AWS was created to meet startups growing demand for IT infrastructure, enabling them to develop their services without securing capital in hardware and software. https://www.youtube.com/watch?v=QVUqyOuNUB8.

the technicality of the solution, without seeing the details of the user experience. But it is the latter that will cause the project to fail or succeed. Asking average users to be part of the proof of concept will bring the vision necessary for its adoption.

2. Integrate security, especially the identification process. If the user needs to have another identity with different username and password from those he uses to access the network, you set aside an essential point of the adoption of the solution. It is essential that the directories are synchronized in one way or another (that is the local and the one in the cloud), to offer a homogeneity of identification. It is possible to strengthen access through the introduction of multifactor authentication for example. Do not add a new digital identity!

3. Limit the proof of concept to a short time. One, maybe two weeks. Testers need to understand that the speed of testing is paramount. It is not once again a pilot project that is likely to end in production. This is a test. Like when your car dealership offers you to test drive the vehicle that has taken your attention. It's not about keeping it a month! Usually, you have it for twenty-four hours. It's up to you to try everything. It's the same with a POC. Test everything quickly and draw conclusions.

When the POC is complete, disable the testers' access. It seems obvious, yet it is seldom done. A POC is indeed, once again, not destined to be put into production. It's out of the question the testers get used to it. They must test, make their assessment, and make suggestions for modification and improvement. It is through these conclusions that it will be possible to define precisely the outlines of the final service.

Once this POC is successful, involve legal. It is indeed crucial to validate the privacy of the users, as well as the protection and the security of the data and applications. The legal department must then be a part of the choice. If the users of the system may not notice that the data and applications are in the cloud, they must be able to be made aware without becoming uncomfortable. The legal department will then be able to make its recommendations and take part in negotiations with the access provider to guarantee the rights of the organization.

The POC may fail. There are many reasons: technical failure, too complex user interface, missing features, etc. It should then be redone or redefined. It is out of question to consider putting into production a solution that users do not want. This is the safest way to reject and abandon the solution in the short or medium term. And if this is your first cloud project, it's a good bet that the cloud will be declared to be responsible, even if it's not. For a first project, you cannot fail, so the POC is of paramount importance.

Once these steps are successful, the signed service contract marks the beginning of the possible production.

Successive small wins rather than a big bang

In terms of IT project management, I am rather an aficionado of the phased deployment, what I call small wins, rather than pressing the switch of the new solution on D-day, the Big Bang approach! The iterative approach, when possible, is far preferable. The implementation of hybrid technologies often allows it. Let's take two examples.

You move the email system in the cloud. Migrate mailboxes, user group by user group, leaving you a few days between each, in order to observe, learn and correct if necessary. Both systems will coexist for a few weeks or months, which will certainly bring you extra work. But this is only a transitional phase. If possible, have the users make the migration by themselves. A vast majority is able to install a new application on their phones. So, they should be able to do the same on their computer if you have developed a complete user manual (online as it should be) and have set up a support line.

You add functionality to an existing software, which is in the cloud. If you can, make the two versions coexist and again deploy by user groups. While data migration may be problematic and cause slowdowns or additional work to replicate data between databases, the game is worth the effort in terms of learning and adoption. Finally, it is easier to put an end to a deployment that has impacted only a small number of individuals rather than the whole organization.

> **Note** Originally developed for software development, the scrum project management method revolves around fast phases called sprints, delivering rapid results by multidisciplinary teams. It is interesting to draw on this method for cloud projects. Indeed, as I indicated earlier, a cloud project is more likely to succeed if it is deployed user group by user group, to learn and correct potential errors on a continuous flow basis. So, we can structure such a project in successive sprints of a few days each. This makes it possible to have a rapid visibility of the advancement by involving all the necessary actors and keeping an open communication.

If you don't see how to cut your project in sprints, go back to the drawing board. Talk to your service provider. Here's for example, the list of responsibilities of the client[71] as part of an Office 365 project managed under FastTrack, the Microsoft Cloud Integration Framework:

- Develop and implement your success plan.
- Provide any enhancements and integrations to your Office 365 tenant beyond the configurable options listed here.
- Provide overall program and project management, including:
  - Assigning a project manager as the primary contact for the FastTrack Manager.
  - Assigning a technical lead as the primary contact for the FastTrack Engineer.
  - Assigning technical resources to perform remediation, configuration, and enablement tasks as outlined by the FastTrack team.
- Provide resources accountable for driving end-user adoption of the service.
- Provide end-user communications, documentation, training, and change management.
- Identify and engage appropriate business sponsors.
- Provide helpdesk documentation and training.
- Produce any reports, presentations, or meeting minutes that are specific to your organization.

---

[71] https://technet.microsoft.com/library/mt651704.aspx

- Create architectural and technical documentation specific to your organization.
- Design, procure, install, and configure hardware and networking.
- Procure, install, and configure software.
- Configure, package, and distribute client software required for Office 365.
- Manage, configure, and apply security policies.
- Activate mobile devices.
- Provide network configuration, analysis, bandwidth validation, testing, and monitoring.
- Alter the network to provide the necessary bandwidth for Skype for Business Online services.
- Manage a technical change management approval process and create supporting documentation.
- Specify and define group policies for user, workstation, and server management.
- Modify your operational model and operation guides.
- Set up multi-factor authentication.
- Decommission and remove source environments (like messaging and collaboration).
- Construct and maintain your test environment.
- Install Lync 2013 or Skype for Business Online 2015 admin tools and service packs to support split domain configuration.
- Install service packs and other required updates on infrastructure servers.
- Provide and configure any public Secure Sockets Layer (SSL) certificates.

And here is a subset of the tasks performed by the FastTrack team. This is only for the evaluation phase[72].

- Hold a success planning call to provide guidance to you for successful user adoption.
- Provide an administrative overview.

---

[72] All the phases of the project decomposed in simple actions can be found here: https://technet.microsoft.com/en-us/library/mt651706.aspx.

- Provide guidance about:
  - DNS, network, and infrastructure needs.
  - Client needs (internet browser, client operating system, mobile device, and services' needs).
  - User identity and provisioning.
  - Enabling eligible services that are purchased and defined as a part of onboarding.
  - Driving successful service adoption and value.
- Establish the timeline for remediation activities.
- Provide a remediation checklist.
- Assess the existing SharePoint Server 2013 or SharePoint Server 2016 infrastructure including:
  - Prerequisites for SharePoint Online Hybrid.
  - On-premises infrastructure readiness for SharePoint Online Hybrid features.
  - Access to required SharePoint Online endpoints.
  - Audiences for OneDrive for Business Hybrid.
- Assess the existing Lync or Skype for Business Online infrastructure including:
  - Supported Skype for Business client deployment strategy.
  - Access to endpoints.
  - Connection quality.
  - Bandwidth estimates.
  - Prerequisites to support split domain server configuration.
  - Readiness of identified users to move onto Skype for Business Online.
- Assess the messaging infrastructure, including:
  - Overall mail flow and routing principles.
  - Client access (including existing published client-access endpoints).
  - Source messaging environment for integration needs.
- Provide data migration if the FastTrack Center data migration service is used and if you meet eligibility.

Nothing very complicated, yet necessary to know, to foresee and to execute. What I appreciate in the above approach is its decomposition into simple actions that can each be the subject of separate and sometimes parallel sprints. A recurring point is that of user adoption. That is the critical point of any project. Without adoption, no success is possible. However, consider that the cloud has nothing to do with it, as we will see now.

Features and benefits

Cloud or not cloud, the success of any project goes through users. If you have made a proof of concept by including some, you have a valuable return of experience. It is thanks to the results of your POC and to the partnership with your service provider that you will be able to fine-tune communication and training for users.

I named this part Features and benefits in memory of my business training. Indeed, as any seller can explain to you, a customer seldom buys features. It's not the leather upholstery, it's the comfort and the smell. This is not the six-cylinder engine, it is the accelerations and purring. These are not the seven modular seats, it is able to charge everything, including children, for holidays. The benefits should, therefore, be emphasized.

We've all met them. They have become obvious to you. Not yet for your users, and it is the latter that will indicate which ones are most important to their eyes:

- Security
- Speed
- Mobility
- Look and feel
- Ease of Use
- Privacy
- etc.

If you integrate the fact that it is a cloud solution, you may be polarizing the intrinsic benefits of the cloud and not the new solution. For example, let's take mobility and email. For a clear majority of users, messaging and mobile computing are unnoticeable. They already consult their Gmail, outlook.com or Yahoo! account on their mobile. Having their professional messaging secure on the same platform will seem to them to be obvious, even a non-event if you already proposed it. However, putting forward that the size of the mailbox is now unlimited or that it is no longer necessary to open a VPN connection will take a different resonance.

So, the idea is to capitalize on what will make life easier for your users, to increase their productivity while benefiting from modern and functional tools. I am always amazed at the gap between the tools offered by the organizations and those available free of charge to the public. We sometimes have the impression of a generation gap, between what was at the forefront of the twentieth century and what should be common in the twenty-first. And this is just the beginning, as the gap widens at high speed with the development of artificial intelligence.

If you think about your users, you should not forget your own suppliers and customers. Your new system will make your employees more productive, your products more innovative or your processes more fluid. Tell it! To the public and to your suppliers and customers. For example, instant messaging in the cloud may allow its federation with those of some of your customers or suppliers. This will amplify the reduction of your communication costs while integrating your customers and suppliers better into your business processes.

It is possible to multiply the examples: integrating ordering process directly into your CRM and your ERP, supervising in real time the sold hardware, as do today companies like ThyssenKrupp or Rolls-Royce that we met in the previous pages, or monitoring and guaranteeing transactions through a blockchain implementation of the traceability of your products.

We all know the phrase "sky is the limit" to indicate that there is virtually no limit to a solution or question. I like this parallel when we talk about cloud because, in essence, a cloud has an elevation limit, yet with the cloud, the sky is the limit. The cloud is not the limit, it's what you can do with it. And that we have not yet achieved is the real potential for innovation.

Capitalize on the first project

Here it is, you're in the cloud. It is almost certain that your project has not gone as planned. Positively or negatively. It is possible that everything was faster, simpler and more fluid than expected, especially if you didn't have an existing system to go back to. It is also possible that everything was more complicated than initially planned: the integration of the directory did not go well because of thousands of orphaned objects, data migration was delayed by a larger than expected volume of corrupted or inaccessible data, or deployment of applications on client workstations encountered unexpected network difficulties.

It is rare for the first cloud project to go one hundred percent as planned. Nothing unusual and nothing of concern. On the contrary! This is the price to pay for discovering all the trade-offs made over the years. These applications that have been acquired, polluting the network. These accounts that have been created, abandoned, now filling the directory. These network links that have been added to satisfy a department, bottlenecking communications.

Note I have seen many early projects going to trash because meeting unexpected difficulties. I remember this client, whose name I will not mention, you will understand why, who wanted to deploy an instant messaging solution and voice over IP. Once the proof of concept parameters was set and the cloud environment was installed, there were only a few clients left to deploy. Almost all PCs were running different and pirated versions of Windows and Office. From Windows XP to Windows 7, from Office 2003 to Office 2013, as many types of anti-virus as from machines, network hubs installed on the floor in some offices. Although the network was tested beforehand, and the Internet connection evaluated in terms of bandwidth and latency, just about anything was in place for a successful POC. The few clients deployed on the main link of the local network worked roughly correctly. On the other hand, the first client deployed on a remote link put an incredibly long time to connect, and the latency was deplorable. Yet the other applications worked well, from the point of view of the IT department. When this POC was finalized, with all the difficulties of the world, users revealed that nothing really worked as expected. They were wasting an infinite time and that they often found alternative solutions with their mobile phone and a 3G connection. The entire network architecture had to be restarted from scratch, homogenize the applications and review the structure of the business directory before launching the first cloud application. The cloud cannot function with mediocrity. Of course, this has influenced the implementation of the solution, which to date, three years after this failed POC, is still not in production.

The cloud does not fit well with application, network or security mediocrity. The verdict is usually immediate: the ultimate slowness. Now the world of IT supports nothing less than slowness. Yet, data centers are massive and allow for virtually unlimited computing power, fiber connections are redundant and ultra-fast, security is enhanced, from encryption to multifactor authentication. When something doesn't work in the cloud, it's ninety-nine percent your fault, and that's one of the reasons for this first project: to make you discover everything that's wrong.

One of the great benefits of the cloud is to be able to measure everything. The definition of metrics for measuring the success of the project is therefore important. This will range from the number of messages processed, the number of clients deployed, the volume of data analyzed to the application utilization rate, the reduction in maintenance times, or the increase in the number of client requests processed per hour. The important thing here is to measure the gains sought and obtained.

It becomes essential to communicate these results to the general management so that we can continue to deploy other applications in the cloud. To do this, a successful strategy is to communicate around three main themes:

1. **Before and after**. Describe the solution in place, with its pros and cons. Describe the new solution, how it eliminates the previous disadvantages and lessons learned during its deployment.
2. **The metrics of success**. Describe the results obtained in quantitative and qualitative terms. If you have included multiple users in the POC, you have a holistic view of the organization that needs to be put forward.
3. **The feedback from users**. A case study and the testimony of the users are ways to direct the light on the subjective gains brought by the project.

These three parts come from the world of sales. It is all about selling the success of this project to allow the following one. Above all, this communication will help to position cloud technologies at the heart of the organization's digital transformation.

A small digression though. Cloud does not always mean public cloud, as we have seen several times. The cloud refers to a set of technologies that apply to the private, community and public cloud. It is, therefore, possible to sell the idea of a private cloud as a positive evolution of an "old generation" data center. These modern technologies make it possible to set up a hybrid cloud-compatible architecture that seems to be the best in the short and medium term. The hybrid cloud provides the dual advantage of modernizing the datacenter while opening it to public cloud services seamlessly and securely. This often helps to reassure the general management that may not be totally comfortable with the idea of being at the mercy of a service provider.

This first successful project is the first step. It remains to define the continuation and evolution of the whole information system and the organization to the cloud. Let us look at this penultimate topic.

Define the Roadmap

Once, the first step concluded successfully, the Yellow Brick Road opens in front of you to the Emerald City of the cloud! You can consider moving into the cloud other systems and why not your entire data center. If the idea makes you wince, know that more and more customers are taking the leap, shedding off all their servers and relying exclusively on public cloud services and direct redundant connectivity.

However, moving a service or a system is one thing, moving several is a whole different project. There are indeed many factors to consider:

- **Cost**. If we have seen that the TCO is generally favorable to the cloud, it is not always the case with aging systems that will have to be updated in the longer term.
- **Technical feasibility**. Any system that has not been designed to operate on a virtual machine, communicate exclusively via an IP network or remotely accessed may not work at all in cloud mode. Even if these rules are not all gold. There is indeed a lot of applications that can work in cloud mode by using software abstraction layers and relying on remote

access through an application like XenApp or XenDesktop[73] of Citrix or Amazon Workspaces[74].

- **Strategic choice**. The organization may decide not to move a system to the public cloud by sheer strategic choice. It may want to keep her hand one hundred percent on how it works.

- **Functional dependencies**. If an application has dependencies to another application to operate, it is quite possible that moving one without the other is not possible. This is, for example, the case of a business intelligence engine that would rely on data from several other systems. Unless you provide ETL (Extraction, Transformation, Loading) mechanisms that move data to a warehouse in the cloud, there is very little chance that the BI application can work with an acceptable level of performance.

- **Access**. As with technical feasibility or functional dependencies, if the architecture of a system has been designed to work on a local network, there is little chance that it will work on a 3G Internet link for example. As a result, universal access may not be necessary or feasible, making the cloudless attractive.

- **Security**. For having had the chance to work with the Strategic Air Forces IT, at the very beginning of its modernization, I learned that confidential information can remain so only if it is on a network that has not a single access point to the outside. Any very secure system can be compromised when there is an access point. This is the case with any cloud system. As Eric Schmidt, the former CEO of Google, once said: "If you have something that you don't want anyone to know, maybe you shouldn't be doing it in the first place". It is the same with information. If you are storing information that you want no one to access, you may already start by not storing it.

This list is not intended to be exhaustive, I recommend you to think about it in depth to ensure that nothing has been forgotten in your analysis. I propose however a simple checklist to help you in the realization of your roadmap.

---

[73] https://www.citrix.com/products/xenapp-xendesktop/
[74] https://aws.amazon.com/workspaces/

1. Start listing all operating systems and software bricks. This goes from the directory to anti-virus to databases and email systems. Each of these bricks is usually identified by a name, a year and a version number. For example, SQL Server 2016 version 13.0.4001.0.

2. With each of these programs, indicate whether, technically, It works in a virtual machine and is supported to work in a public cloud. In case of doubt, the vendor may be able to tell you and in case it does not provide an answer, the public cloud provider will be able to guarantee it or not.

3. List all your applications running in your datacenter. These are the applications that rely on software bricks, such as the CRM, the ERP or the HRIS. Also, indicate the year and the version number.

4. In the same way that you indicated for the software bricks if they were operating in public cloud, do the same for each of these programs. Here again, the vendor or the public cloud provider will be able to tell you. Attention However on this point, publishers may not play the game. Oracle For example or SAP might warn you they won't support instances of their programs on clouds other than their own. It is no longer a question of pure technical feasibility, but of software support on the part of the vendors. These are practices that tend to disappear, but unfortunately still exist. Don't let yourself be intimidated! This is only a technical feasibility at this stage.

5. At this point, pick up these two lists and note in front of each application, which ones it depends on. For example, the CRM will be dependent on the database software, enterprise messaging, and the data warehouse. This step is important because it will provide you with a guide in the application migration order, as well as an indication of which ones will need to be migrating at the same time.

6. Last but one step: pick up the list of all the applications that can't be moved to the cloud. Note the reasons and the possible solutions. This can go to the simple drop off of the application because it's the end of life, for example, to its update to a more modern version or to a pure and hard change.

7. The final step before the creation of a full roadmap is the sorting of the list. This is certainly the most difficult step, not technically, but organizationally. In fact, we will have to establish priority criteria. Knowing that the evolution of technologies and their availability will

undoubtedly be the troublemaker. It is difficult to predict where cloud service providers are going, what technologies are going to be important and which ones are going to be abandoned. However, because change is natural, your roadmap will evolve. To help you with the sorting of applications, I propose five evaluation criteria:

- o **Availability**. Are the application and its dependencies available? It is possible that the availability is partial, for example, if only the last version of a dependency is supported while the application is running on an earlier version. You will have to go through several tests before you can validate the availability of the solution in cloud mode.
- o **Cost**. Consider all costs, including those for updating applications or bandwidth and training users if any. An assessment is enough at this point.
- o **Impact**. The impact can be multifaceted. How many users are affected, is the application critical to the operation of the organization, etc.
- o **Migration**. Depending on the technical criteria and a possible POC, is migration expected to be easy or difficult?
- o **Adoption**. Are you considering evolutions in usage? How is adoption perceived? Simple and fast or difficult and slow.

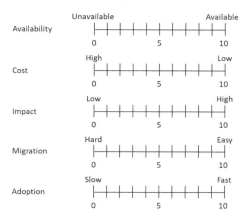

Figure 7-3 - Priority criteria

Each criterion is evaluated on a scale of 0 to 10 as indicated in Figure 7-3 - Priority criteria. It is then sufficient to add the value given to each criterion to obtain a score of 0 to 50. 50 indicates a candidate application to the cloud. 0, on the other hand, indicates an application that is likely to remain local.

You can then transfer all your results in a table like the one illustrated by Table 7-1 - List of applications to migrate to the cloud, sorting it in descending order of precedence (attention, the highest number indicates the highest priority).

Application	Year	Version	Cloud	Dependencies	Priority
			Y/N		
			Y/N		
			Y/N		
			Y/N		

Table 7-1 - List of applications to migrate to the cloud

When you come to this milestone, you are one of the few percents of the organizations that looked at its adoption of the cloud seriously. It remains to define a time scale for all of these projects, to make a Gantt chart and to communicate its effects to the general management for validation of both the vision and the budgets to be associated with it.

It will then involve all the stakeholders in the company, from sales to human resources, from communication to general management. As we have seen over these pages, the cloud is not a computer geek's whim. It deeply disrupts the structures of organizations and their functioning. Without the positive support of all, its adoption is doomed to failure. Ready?

Get Started

When you have a gold hand in poker and you are sure to win, you can "all-in" bet all your chips. This is all about "either it makes or breaks". Knowing that if you have followed the steps that we have previously seen, there is little risk that it will break and all the chances that it will make. However, the idea of "all-in" is the lack of backward step and the total involvement of everyone.

I insist heavily on this notion of total involvement. The cloud and its associated technologies are currently perceived as the fourth Industrial Revolution (see page 177). The future will tell us if that is indeed the case. In the meantime, the examples abound in the sense of a rapid transformation of the organizations that adopt it. Innovation has always been the driving force behind the evolution of organizations. The one pushed by the cloud is no different. It is seen in all sectors of society.

In most cases, the failure of a cloud project is not due to technology, but to a lack of visibility, communication, and involvement. There is a technical component at the origin of the failure. This may be a lack of bandwidth, a component that is not functional in a virtual environment or a dependency that had been poorly studied. However, with the implication of all, an acceptance of the consequences and a clear vision of the benefits, these pitfalls can be circumvented, and the project moves forward.

I only have one recommendation to close this chapter: Stop thinking and start!

What do we do now?

Conclusion

"Bloody revolution can never solve our problems. Only a profound inward revolution which alters all our values can create a different environment, an intelligent social structure, and such a revolution can be brought about only by you and me. No new order will arise until we individually break down our own psychological barriers and are free."

Education and the Significance of Life, Jiddu Krishnamurti

When I started this book, at the beginning of the year 2017, I did not know that it was going to be that difficult to write. It's been almost ten years since I started to "evangelize" Cloud technologies for Microsoft across Africa. I had been confronted with the worst and the best. I had seen clients thinking I'm mad and others to be amazed at so much power at their fingertips. I had seen failed projects miserably by cruel lack of preparedness and others deployed in a few weeks successfully. In a few words, I had lived Hell, Paradise, and Purgatory from customer to customer, from amazed smiles in Kinshasa to smirk ones in Accra.

I tried to condense these ten years in the pages that preceded. These ten years have also marked the 30's of my professional life in IT if I include the eighteen months spent in the French Strategic Air Force Command (COFAS). The period during which, we, my friends and myself, participated actively in its computerization by programming video cards in assembler (it was before Windows 3.1) in order to be able to display the flight plans, the weather and other parameters to the commanding officers in real time.

In thirty years, the Internet has changed the world. At the end of the 80's, almost no one had an email address. In 2017, it would seem incongruous if you don't. And don't even mention a Facebook account, like more than two billion people on the planet. Between email and Facebook, we better understand the stakes and the risks. The email is used to make purchases online, to receive its tax return and tomorrow could become our electronic ID card, our bank account or our passport number (an email address is, in fact, one of the only universally unique identifiers). On the other side, Facebook knows all about us, of our activities, of what we like or not, of the sites we consult, of the people we frequent, casting doubt on the use that can be made of this personal information.

But the biggest revolution, relying on internet technologies, is cloud computing. This ability to consume almost unlimited online resources by paying only what is used, or even paying nothing in the cases of certain consumer services, is the real revolution that allowed the service industry, the creation of new industrial empires and the profound change in our societies. In 2017, we can say that nothing will be like before the cloud.

Of course, the cloud is not free of danger, it is mostly rich with promises. And we are only at the beginning. The years ahead of us will expose us to new services, new technologies, new businesses that are still in the incubation labs. How many Tesla, Facebook or Uber will pop up? How to create today's cloud tomorrow?

This book is only a very small contribution in view of the immense challenges facing Africa and other emerging countries. But if it allows one or two companies to be created, to reinvent themselves or to develop then, it will have achieved its objective. In the next five years, Amazon, Google, Microsoft, SAP, IBM, and others will continue to invest in data centers, connectivity, and services to enable the largest number of organizations to benefit from this incredible adventure that is the cloud!

The question is no longer whether to go to the cloud. It is no longer when it is necessary to go. It is where to start? As we have seen in Chapter 7, What do we do now? there is an urgent need to choose this project and get started. The risks are much less today than they were ten years ago when the first organizations were testing the water. Of course, the path may be full of humpbacks and potholes, but no one has ever said that there was none on the yellow brick road of the land of Oz. With reflection, preparation and flexibility, you will spend an incredible moment and launch your organization in the future! What are you waiting for? Close this book and get started!

Bon voyage!

Conclusion

Appendices

Virtual Server offers

Not always easy to find in the offers of virtual machines. Which machine to choose for what use. This List can help you.

Use	Use type	Microsoft	Aws	Google	Ovh
General	Development and testing servers, low-traffic Web servers, small and medium-scale databases, proof-of-concept servers, code repositories.	A	T2	N1-Standard	B2

Use	Use type	Microsoft	Aws	Google	Ovh
General perfor-mance	Most applications, relational databases, in-memory caching and analytics, SharePoint, back-end SAP.	D, D v2	M4, M3	F1	C2
Inten-sive calcu-lation	Batch processing, web servers, analytics et gaming	F	C4, C3	N1-HIGHCPU	C2
Memory	Large SQL and NoSQL databases, as well as ERP solutions, SAP and SAP HANA, Data storage.	G	X1, R4, R3	N1-Highmem	R2
High perfor-mance	High-Performance computing, batch processing, analytical, molecular and fluid dynamics modeling, financial analysis.	H	X1, P2, F1	Custom	G1
Storage	NoSQL databases, such as Cosmos DB, Cassandra, MongoDB, Cloudera, and	L	I3, D2	Custom	R2

Use	Use type	Microsoft	Aws	Google	Ovh
	Redis. In-memory database, data warehousing applications, and large transactional databases.				
Graphic	Graphic rendering, video editing, remote visualization, high performance, and analytics computing.	N	P2, C4, C3, F1	Custom	G1

Table A-1 - Virtual Server offers

As you can see in the Table A-1 - Virtual Server offers, service providers seem to find clever to define different nomenclatures for their offers. Where this gets complicated is that Amazon and Microsoft have overlapping offers. Thus, the H or N machines at Microsoft and P2 and F1 at AWS are interchangeable. This creates a bit of the Chinese Restaurant menu syndrome: Too many choices kill he choice.

However, it is important to understand the primary function of the machine you want to put online. With prices ranging from a few cents to several hundreds of dollars a day, the choice of the machine is paramount, as well as its use. I have for example seen customers forgetting to stop test machines and be billed several thousand dollars a month, where they should actually pay only a few dozens of dollars. Thus, sizing and duration of use are criteria to be considered. This will have an influence on your ROI calculations, as we have seen in Chapter 1, The cloud, this beautiful Nebula.

Artificial intelligence and machine learning offers

It is the topic that is much talked about and is the fruit of all the wildest speculations and forecasts since Stephen Hawking and Elon Musk have warned mankind against the risks of the singularity. This ultimate moment when the machine becomes more intelligent than man[75]. However, whether we like it or not, the services of artificial intelligence (AI) and machine learning are well present and available to everyone. The following list is far from exhaustive in particular because of the rapid evolution of technologies and the availability of services. The computing power required for these services makes them the turf of the very big providers, although we see some niche startups appearing. The following pages are therefore focused on the "big four" that are Microsoft, AWS, Google, and IBM, and I cite some of the niche players

Still image analysis

Recognizing a celebrity, classifying a photo, filtering an image, all possible actions with image recognition services. The fashion industry has been using them for some time now: Take a picture of a garment, worn or not, and find it in an online store!

Company	Service Name	Features
Microsoft	Computer Vision API	Able to read text in an image, including manuscript. Automatic generation of miniatures.
Microsoft	Face API and Emotion API	Face Identification, search for similarities, grouping of faces. Emotion Detection.
Microsoft	Personalized Vision Service	Learning Service from template (default integrated by other vendors)
Aws	Amazon Rekognition	Advanced Facial analysis. Automatic moderation.
Google	Cloud Vision API	Detection of texts, logos, and faces.
IBM	Watson Visual Recognition	

Table A-2 – Fixed Image Analysis Services

---

[75] An excellent read on singularity and the future of mankind: Homo Deus: A Brief History of Tomorrow, https://www.harpercollins.com/9780062464316/homo-deus.

These services are constantly evolving, as new images are continuously loaded on the web through systems like the Amazon online store, Flickr or OneDrive services, to name a few. Here are illustrated, some of the features of these APIs, which can be included in any application with only a few lines of code.

It is possible to classify photos for example to recognize a face or the main elements of a photo. The first step is to recognize the simple characteristics: Is it a woman or a man? In what age range? Figure A-1 gives an example.

Figure A-1 - Face recognition (from Microsoft's face API)

The system will analyze the characteristics of a photo and associated statistics, as shown in Figure A-2, from Amazon's Rekognition API. It then becomes possible to index an image with strong degrees of certainty. This indexing will then allow you to search, like the ones you probably do with Google or Bing to find an image to illustrate a PowerPoint presentation for example.

Figure A-2 - Recognition of the elements of an image (Amazon Rekognition API)

Because they analyze the characteristics of the images, these APIs will allow us to go further, for example, associating multiple images with each other or identifying an individual. The association will make it possible to find similar people in a group. The identification will, for instance, allow to find the same person in a crowd from a source picture.

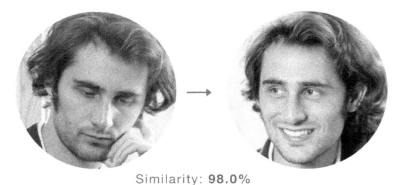

Similarity: **98.0%**

Figure A-3 - Person Identification (Amazon Rekognition API)

In the same way, it will be possible to recognize a celebrity, whether an image is accessible to any person or is of adult nature (violence, sex, etc.). The Vision APIs classifies the image from its main characteristics. In Figure A-4, the Vision

API tells us with 98% of certainty that this is a photo of kitesurfing (although you cannot see the kite itself), which will also allow extracting some Web entities (vacation, sea, kitesurfing, etc.) in a table to generate an index.

Figure A-4 - Analysis of a picture on the fly thanks to the Google Vision API

Many companies now use these services, like Uber for example, which uses the Microsoft facial recognition API to identify the driver of its vehicles and ensure that it is the driver in question. This allows the company to strengthen its security by guaranteeing the identity of the drivers.

Video analysis

Indexing, classifying and searching for videos, the Holy Grail of any collection of documents. With the volume of videos produced these days, these tasks can be incredibly time-consuming when they are simply humanly possible. With the services of artificial intelligence, they become possible.

Company	Service Name	Features
Microsoft	Video Indexer and video API	Detection and indexing of spoken words, faces, and emotions. Automatic thumbnail generation. Stabilization of the videos.
Google	Cloud Video Intelligence API	Indexing and querying video catalogs on the fly.

Table A-3 - Video Analysis Services

The main service offered by the artificial intelligence APIs dedicated to video is their indexing. They allow to automatically put words on videos to facilitate the search. If you go to Bing or Google and do a video search from words as illustrated in the figure below, you will get a list of videos indexed against those words.

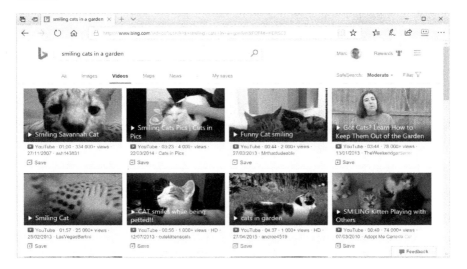

Figure A-5 - Search for videos in Bing

This indexing was done automatically. But we can go a little further. In the figure above, you notice that in the upper right corner, the search has a filter called "Moderate", so it does not return any video that can be classified as "Adult". The video API allows the content to be moderated automatically.

Indexing also makes it possible, like still image analysis APIs, to recognize faces and analyze feelings. The following picture, extracted from the Microsoft Video API user's manual, gives us an overview of the results obtained. Although the face of the fourth person of the video is unknown, it is known that it appeared 43% of the time. We also find the keywords of the indexing and the general feeling of the video.

This will allow not only its archiving and make it possible to search it, but also trigger workflows or various tasks depending on the content.

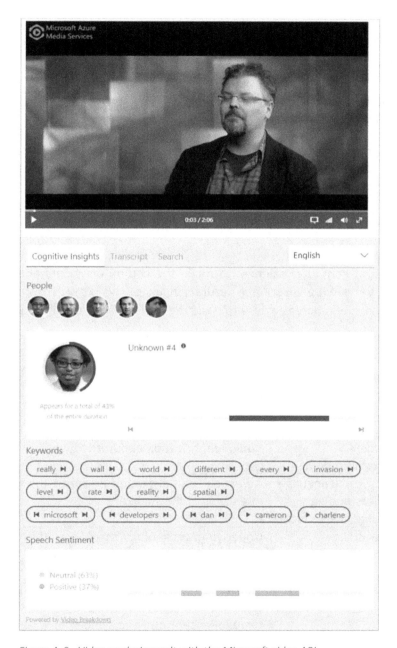

Figure A-6 - Video analysis result with the Microsoft video API

The Microsoft API allows going one step further by allowing the transcription of the spoken soundtrack. At the time of writing this book, it automatically recognizes English, French, Spanish, German, Italian, Simplified Chinese, Brazilian Portuguese, Japanese and Russian. It becomes possible for example to automatically subtitle a video, in the viewer's language, since the video API also allows on-the-fly translation in the languages indicated above.

Microsoft also automatically allows you to extract the text contained in videos, to separate the spoken soundtrack from the rest of the sounds and music present. Coupled with streaming services, the video APIs allow the implementation of systems for the dissemination of corporate videos, or online training for example.

Speech recognition

Another Holy Grail of computer science: to make the computer understand what it is told and to have it answering in natural language. This is much more complex than it seems, but increasingly within the reach of artificial intelligence in the cloud.

Company	Service Name	Features
Microsoft	Speech Bing API	Transcription of voice to text and text to voice.
Microsoft	Personalized Voice Service	Creating templates to respond to different contexts.
Microsoft	Speaker Recognition API	Audio Identification and Authentication
Microsoft	LUIS (Language Understanding Intelligence Service)	A Service to analyze and interpret the intentions of the speaker.
AWS	Amazon Lex	Underlying technology to Alexa, the Amazon chatbot service, allowing to analyze the intentions of the speaker.
Aws	Amazon Polly	Transcribes text into voice in more than twenty languages considering the regional accent and the gender of the speaker.
Google	API Cloud Speech	Context personalization. Automatic noise filtering. 80 supported languages.

Company	Service Name	Features
Google	Cloud Natural Language API	Analyzes the structure and meaning of the text.
IBM	Natural Language Understanding	Retrieving metadata from unstructured data. Understanding of feelings. 9 Supported languages.

Table A-4 - Voice recognition Services

The world of speech recognition is boiling and constantly improving. It makes possible other services like on-the-fly translation. For instance, Google and Microsoft offer APIs, respectively API Cloud Translation, and API Translator Text, allowing to translate text on the fly with success rates now superior to human translators.

As you can see from the two examples below, the transcription is not perfect at 100%: Google has confused the French conjunction "et" with the verb "est", Microsoft has forgotten the article "Il" of the second sentence. However, an analysis through a grammatical and orthographic corrector should overcome these small errors. For the moment the Microsoft spelling API only deals with English, and the other large publishers do not offer any to my knowledge.

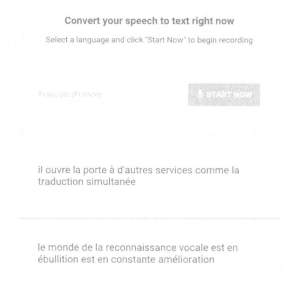

Figure A-7 - Automatic Transcription of the voice API from Google

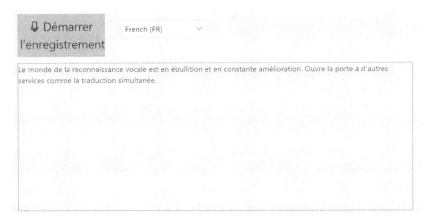

Figure A-8 - Automatic Transcription with the Microsoft Speech recognition API

One of the fascinating aspects of artificial intelligence, however, is not to be able to transcribe the language of speakers but to understand their intentions. For example, when I ask Alexa to play my favorite song of the moment, the system must understand that I want to listen to music and that the music I am looking for is my favorite song. Lex from Amazon, Cloud Natural language from Google, Watson Natural Language Understanding from IBM and LUIS from Microsoft are services that allow you to understand the user's intentions and potentially act on orders given.

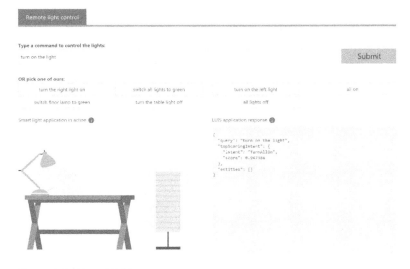

Figure A-9 - Use of LUIS

226

The above figure is a demonstrator of LUIS from Microsoft. Relatively simple, however, it contains ambiguities. Indeed, if I ask to turn on the light, should we turn on all the lamps? Just one? Which one? You can remove all the ambiguities by asking, for example, to turn on all the lights. LUIS allows you to interpret the user's intentions by calculating a confidence index. In the example above, the intention is to turn on the lights, with a confidence index of 94.7%. Because no entity has been detected (the command does not apply to a defined lamp), LUIS, therefore, decides to apply the order to each light.

If we had asked to turn on in green the left lamp, LUIS would have generated the following interpretation:

```
{  {
   "Query": "Switch floor lamp to green",
   "TopScoringIntent": {
     "Intent": "Turnn",
     "score": 0.9932177
   },
   "Entities": [
     {
        "Entity": "Floor",
        "Type": "Light",
        "StartIndex": 7,
        "endIndex": 11,
        "Resolution": null,
        "Score": 0.995927334
     },
     {
        "Entity": "Green",
        "type": "Color",
        "startIndex": 21,
        "Turkeys": 25,
        "Resolution": null,
        "Score": 0.9996085
     }
   ]
}
```

The order is, therefore, to turn on the light, but this time adding two entities: This is the lamp located on the ground, entity "floor", and the green color, entity "green". We also see that the confidence index of these two entities is close to 100%.

These services are built on learning engines that will allow the system to improve over time.

Search

Search made Google's fortune. However, Microsoft and Amazon open their APIs to search online or on specific domains documents, pictures and videos that you want to expose to your users.

Company	Service Name	Features
Microsoft	API Bing Search	Microsoft provides specialized APIs for suggestion, searches in news feeds, images, and video, as well as simple, ad-free search services.
Aws	Amazon CloudSearch	Geolocated, 34 supported languages.

Table A-5 - Search Services

Search is one of the most used functions on the web. It has become an integral part of our digital lives. Microsoft and Amazon APIs provide your users with search capabilities within your applications while benefiting from advanced features.

It is possible to restrict the search area (for example, restrict to searches in French), to integrate automatic filling when entering the searched terms or to search for sites, images, videos or entities, among other features.

The following figure shows the result of a search on the US domain (en-us), applying a strict filter, i.e. eliminating the results for adults, but without applying a time restriction, thus by returning all results irrespective of their dates of creation, and by returning all types of possible results, websites, images, videos, etc.

It is then possible for a developer to retrieve the result as a JavaScript Object Notation (JSON) structure to expose it to the user.

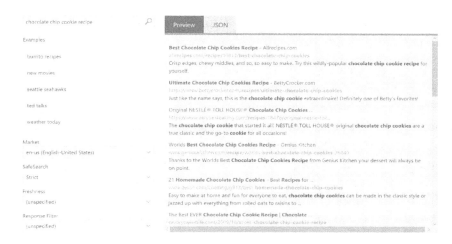

Figure A-10 – Microsoft API Bing Search

These two APIs support several languages and are kept up to date. Unless you want to redevelop your own search engine (good luck), using these APIs will save you valuable resources, while guaranteeing you a professional result.

Recommendations

The champion of recommendations is Amazon. If you searched for an item on the Amazon commerce site, you may have been presented the list of choices of other internet users who searched for the same object. If they appear to be simple, the recommendations are complex and substantially increase the turnover of any commercial company. Those services exist with just some personalization to meet your own needs.

Society	Service Name	Features
Microsoft	Recommendations Service (The Recommendations API is coming end of life in February 2018)	Analysis of joint purchases and purchase history.

Table A-6 - Recommendations Services

The recommendations solutions are narrow artificial intelligence, based on a shopping history, create models using predefined algorithms and use these models to make recommendations to customers based on their choices. We come to propose recommendations such as:

1. Users who enjoyed this product also appreciated these.
2. Depending on your previous purchases, we recommend these products.

In a simplistic way, such a solution can feel easy. However, if the underlying mechanics are complex, their implementations are complex too and depend on the quality and volume of the model data. For example, the Microsoft Recommendations Solution documentation recommends having at least twenty times more transactions than products in your catalog so you can create a quality model. If you have a thousand references in your catalog, you will need at least twenty thousand transactions to make useful recommendations. Here we touch the importance of the quality and the necessary volume of the data so that the AI engines operate correctly. With too low a volume or poor data quality, the recommendations may be erroneous and have a more negative effect on the future behavior of the users.

However, if you have an interesting set of data, you will need to store it at a location where the API can access it, and then start the model creation function. Once this template is created (depending on the size of the dataset, it can take a few minutes to several hours), it is possible to call it to get recommendations.

The following example, taken from the documentation of the Microsoft Recommendations Solution, available from GitHub, sends the product reference 70322 and receives product recommendations reference 46846, 46845 and 41607, with their confidence indices.

Query:

```
GET
https://<service_name>azurewebsites.net/api/models/e16198c
0-3a72-4f4d-b8ab-
e4c07c9bccdb/recommend?itemId=70322</service_name>
X-API-key: Your_api_key
Content-Type: application/JSON
```

Result:

```
[{
        "RecommendedItemId": "46846",
        "Score": 0.45787626504898071
},
{
```

```
        "RecommendedItemId": "46845",
        "Score": 0.12505614757537842
},
...
{
        "RecommendedItemId": "41607",
        "Score": 0.049780447036027908
}]
```

The above example is relatively simple. It is indeed possible to invoke the model with more complex parameters, such as the user's purchase history. The system will then make a cross analysis between the recommendations of the currently chosen product, those previously purchased and all the transactions of the model. We then refine the result to get even closer to the taste of the customer. These formidable recommendations engines have a very positive effect on the commercial results of companies like Amazon. They are now available to smaller companies.

Chatbots

Chatbots (conversational robots) or how to make you believe that a human is listening to you. The chatbots are becoming more and more part of your daily life. They are replacing the first level support services quickly. Coupled with recognition and voice Restitution APIs, Chatbots are becoming call centers agents.

Société	Service Name	Features
Microsoft	Azure Bot Service	Native integration with other Microsoft IA services, including serverless functions.
Aws	Amazon Lex	Native Voice management. Integration with other Amazon services.
Google	API.AI - DialogFlow	API.AI is the Google API allowing the development of conversational interfaces. The DialogFlow company at the origin of this API was purchased by Google in 2016.
IBM	Watson Conversation	Advanced Security.

Table A-7 - Chatbots Services

Who has not reached the Frequently Asked Questions page on a website looking for information? Each time, the experience is similar: we find ourselves in front of a list of questions, but never exactly the one we want. With a conversation robot, this experience can be radically transformed.

By using your FAQ as the source of the chatbot, you develop a primitive version of your robot. By adding search features, you open the world of the web to him. By grafting functions of human conversations, like LUIS, Polly or Cloud Speech, you give it a human varnish. Finally, by linking it to a business API, you allow it to take orders.

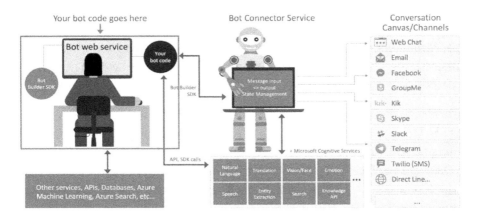

Figure A-11 - Structure of a conversational robot (adapted from the Microsoft Bot Framework documentation)

Intelligent conversational robot construction is made possible by the aggregation of various knowledge channels. It is easy to imagine the power of a conversational robot connected to all available sources of knowledge. However, it is not the most "intelligent" robot that wins, but the one most suited to the search for a user. for example, if a user searches for the operating hours of your store, it will be pointless and counterproductive to provide explanations on the average operating hours of all stores in the area. In the same way, if this same robot knows how to speak as Shakespeare wrote, it will probably not be of great use to the research invoked. Microsoft provides four key questions to the success of a conversational robot:

1. Does the bot easily solve the user's problem with the minimum number of steps?
2. Does the bot solve the user's problem better/easier/faster than any of the alternative experiences?
3. Does the bot run on the devices and platforms the user cares about?
4. Is the bot discoverable? Do the users naturally know what to do when using it?

This seems common sense and should guide any development of conversational robot. None of these questions deals with the pure intelligence or the vast knowledge of the robot, but they all focus on the user experience.

The world of conversational robots is only in its infancy. The progress of the interpretation of the emotions, intentions, and subtleties of conversations will come to these robots and make them become more "intelligent" to the point of thinking they are human beings. Having witnessed this progress, I also predicted the loss of human call center services in the next ten years. The call center operator job is soon endangered!

Machine Learning

When you think about it, you realize that learning is the basis of all knowledge. It is, therefore, necessary to set up the heuristics needed for learning, and then let the machine learn. Simple to explain, ultra-complex to implement, including with the services below.

The previous pages in this appendix gave you an overview of the artificial intelligence capabilities of cloud services. The ultimate step is learning. Recently the AlphaGo Zero AI[76], from the company DeepMind, a subsidiary of Google, learned the game of Go by itself, starting from the rules and arriving in twenty-one days to beat the version of AlphaGo Master, who had beaten the greatest champions of Go. What is interesting here is this notion of learning. AlphaGo Zero had only the knowledge of the basic rules of the game of Go and had only the goal to learn to play to win. Using a deep AI and neural networks, AlphaGo opens the way to the fascinating world of superhuman intelligence, necessary to discover the drugs, energies or materials of tomorrow.

---

[76] https://deepmind.com/blog/alphago-zero-learning-scratch/

Company	Service Name	Features
Microsoft	Machine Learning	Possibility to use R or Python. The foundation of Cortana.
AWS	Amazon Machine Learning	The foundation of Alexa and of the operation of the Amazon site (fraud detection, supply management, ...)
Google	Cloud Machine Learning Engine	Is based on TensorFlow, an Open Source framework for Machine Learning. The basis of Google Photos and Google Cloud Speech.
IBM	Watson	The IBM Machine Learning service from which all other IA services are derived.

Table A-8 - Machine Learning Services

However, without going up to the computational power necessary for this learning of the game of Go, AI and machine learning are available today. Machine learning would require an entire book as the subject is vast and complex. Nevertheless, I go through the basics in the following pages to give you, I hope, the desire to learn more.

Learning machine is based on learning models. These models are in fact data sets, usually massive, that attempt to explain a behavior. Let's take an example I like: cycling balance. To know how to ride a bike, you have to learn to balance yourself on the bike while moving. Basically, you have to integrate three basic movements:

1. Pedal to create and maintain the speed of the bike.
2. Turn the handlebars slightly to turn and create a force that is contrary to gravity when necessary.
3. Move your own body to counterbalance gravity that tends to pull us down.

If we were to cover our bike and the rider with sensors measuring horizontal and vertical speeds, and accelerations, as well as the position of the bike and the rider, we would create a digital model that could be used to teach a robot how to ride a bike. This is what our brain and sensor network (eyes, inner ear, etc.) do, accumulating experience during our attempts to master the craft and stop falling.

Machine learning engines do not do things differently (novelty with AlphaGo Zero is that DeepMind has demonstrated that an AI can learn alone without prior human experience, which opens a whole new field to AI, but this is another topic outside the scope of this book). So, we start from a data set that will make it possible to infer a numerical model from which we will be able to generate a behavior or at least a forecast. Basically, to take our example of learning the bike, it comes down to understand that if I turn the handlebars right and I do not have enough speed or that I am poorly positioned, I will fall if I do not put the right foot on the ground. This seems logical to any human being who knows how to ride a bike, but it is the whole basis of the numerical models and decisions derived from machine learning.

Once the mechanics are put into place, it becomes possible to constantly feed it with new experiments, to refine the models. This logic is used, for example, to detect real-time fraud attempts, to determine the results of marketing campaigns to choose the one that will have the most impact or to define a commercial target in relation to a propensity to buy a product or service.

If all this seems simple and logical in appearance, the implementation is complex. This is one of the reasons why many voices have been raised regarding AI bias. Because the models are generated by human beings, which each possess cognitive bias. Thus, without knowing it, it is possible to introduce into a model a bias that will then make that the AI and its related decisions will be aligned with this bias. For example, favor or exclude a type of behavior, without any reasons other than the model designer bias. This is one of the risks that all serious players in machine learning seek to eliminate.

Machine learning is based on many mathematical algorithms, from Poisson regression to anomaly detection based on Principal Component Analysis (PCA), through bi-class neural networks. It is obviously not my point to deepen these notions, but to give you an idea of the science behind machine learning. You probably understand better why a data scientist is needed to implement big data and machine learning projects.

Figure A-12 - Azure Machine Learning Studio and a credit risk detection model

The previous figure represents part of a credit risk detection model for a financial institution in Azure Machine Learning Studio. Azure Machine Learning Studio is a visual and collaborative development tool for creating, testing, and deploying predictive analytics solutions in the cloud.

Such a solution is composed of several steps, ranging from reading data to processing them, running anomaly detection algorithms or invoking code developed in Python or R. Azure ML Studio allows you to create predictive analysis models that can be deployed as a Web service. They then benefit from the computing power, the elasticity and the safety of Azure.

The solution illustrated in the above figure is described, as well as its implementation in the experiences of the site of the "Cortana Intelligence Gallery", https://gallery.cortanaintelligence.com. This site contains many pre-packaged solutions of artificial intelligence and provides a great way to deepen machine learning mechanisms.

Another way to understand the mechanisms of machine learning is to use Azure ML Workbench to develop machine learning models and deploy them in the form of Docker container, for example.

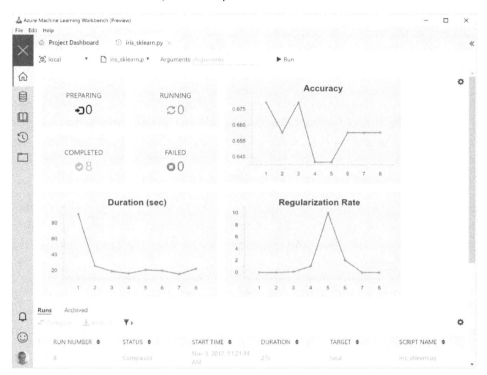

Figure A-13 - Creating a digital model in Azure Machine Learning Workbench

Azure ML Workbench allows the implementation of numerical models, basis of many real-life solutions, such as predictive maintenance, detecting and changing a mechanical or electronic component before it fails, or forecasting customers churn, according to their behavior, allowing to influence commercial policies to reduce the number of such un-registration.

Once these models are developed, they can be queried and expose their results to users to improve decision making. All of these tools and algorithms are rapidly evolving, but not without many ethical and legal problems.

As I often like to remind it, in case of an accident caused by an autonomous car, who is responsible? The owner of the car, its designer or the computer that drives it. If it is the latter, how can we impose a penalty on a machine? If it can make you smile at first glance, we quickly realize that this type of problem is not yet solvable. For this reason, a majority of scientists and AI professionals are now investing in projects that make AI safer and ensure that it is exclusively confined to the benefit of mankind.

The blockchain, the ultimate cloud service

With artificial intelligence, the most discussed topic of information technology is undoubtedly the blockchain. For many, it's just a common name[77]. Yet it contains the power of a radical transformation of vast parts of our lives. The blockchain is a technology for storing and transmitting information, transparently, securely and operating without central control.

The blockchain was made famous thanks to its very first implementation: Bitcoin[78]. Despite its dark side, Bitcoin has paved the way for other cryptocurrencies and has mainly exposed to the public its underlying technology, the blockchain.

One can, therefore, consider a chain of blocks as a tamper-proof accounting book consulted by all the actors of the chain. It is tamper-proof, because of the hashing techniques used, making almost impossible to modify a transaction once validated and included in a block of the chain.

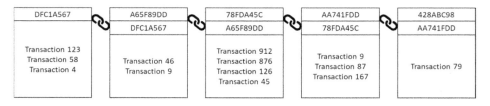

Figure A-14 – A blockchain

Each block in a chain contains Five Elements:

- One or many transactions;

---

[77] https://en.wikipedia.org/wiki/Blockchain
[78] Https://en.wikipedia.org/wiki/Bitcoin

- A unique identifier obtained by hashing its content (a hash is a mathematical function);
- The previous block ID (except for the first block of the chain);
- The measure of the amount of work it was necessary to provide to validate the block;
- A timestamp;

The key feature of the block is its identifier, which is the result of calculating a hash function. Such a function produces a single result depending on the source (the risk of collision, i.e. obtaining the same result from two different sources, is almost nil). The contents of the block are therefore used to calculate its identifier. Each time a new block is created and then added to the chain, it receives the identifier from the previous block after which it was added, increasing the size of the chain. The Figure A-14 — Figure A-14 — A blockchain shows a chain consisting of 5 blocks containing various transactions.

If the contents of a validated block were to be modified (voluntarily or not), its identifier would be changed, the broken chain indicating a change in the block. It's the tamper-proof side of the chain. The existence of a copy of the block then allows to restore it. This is the distributed side of the chain.

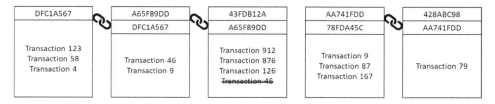

Figure A-15 - Altered block, broken chain

Considering the blockchain illustrated by the Figure A-14 — Figure A-14 — A blockchain. A change to block three is performed by deleting transaction 45. One can imagine a deliberate change made by a criminal who tries to erase his footsteps. The Figure A-15 - Altered block, broken chain illustrates the result. Because the contents of the block are modified, its identifier is also changed (here it goes from 78FDA45C to 43FDB12A), breaking the chain, since the next block contains its former identifier. It will then be possible to return the block to its original state from one of the replicas of the chain since the chain replicates itself to preserve its integrity.

The simple and tamper-proof structure of a blockchain is of interest to many industries, far beyond the cryptocurrencies. Money transfer, insurance, logistics chain, traceability, smart contracts are all areas of interest to the blockchain.

As I wrote in the title of this appendix, the blockchain is the ultimate cloud service, because it can only exist in the cloud and through the cloud. It is the network of networks which allows to store the chain and to validate the blocks (the miners put their computing power at disposal in exchange for a remuneration in the case of cryptocurrencies for example). It is the network of networks that allows managing the replication.

If the theory is simple, the implementation is not. Because of its growing popularity, blockchain also attracts investment and access providers are not left out. Microsoft now offers Blockchain as a Service[79] And Amazon just announced it at the time of the finalization of this book. It is now possible to launch and test a blockchain project without having to build the entire underlying infrastructure.

A final note to this introduction to the blockchain, as the ultimate cloud service. Contrary to many of the ideas received and conveyed, all the blockchains are not public. There are private ones. It is, therefore, possible to implement peer-to-peer services that are only known to its participants. One thing is certain, the story of the blockchain started in 2008 with the birth of Bitcoin and is only at its beginning. There is a strong bet that it is not ready to stop anytime soon.

---

[79] https://azure.microsoft.com/en-us/solutions/blockchain/

www.ingramcontent.com/pod-product-compliance
Lightning Source LLC
LaVergne TN
LVHW022307060326
832902LV00020B/3325

9 781981 094196